JESUS,

a Love Like No Other!

MARY BERRY

WESTBOW°
PRESS
A DIVISION OF THOMAS NELSON
& ZONDERVAN

Unless otherwise noted, all Scripture quotations are taken from the Holman Christian Standard Bible, Copyright 1999, 2000, 2002, 2003, 2009 by Holman Bible Publishers. Used by permission. Holman Christian Standard Bible, Holman CSB, and HCSB are federally registered trademarks of Holman Bible Publishers. All rights reserved.

Scriptures quotations marked NCV are taken from The Holy Bible, New Century Version, copyright 2005 by Thomas Nelson, Inc. Used by permission. All rights reserved

Excerpts taken from Andrew Murray on Prayer by Andrew Murray. Copyright © 1998 by Whitaker House. Used by permission of Whitaker House. www.whitakerhouse.com.

Author Photo used by permission by Lorissa Brunk, September 27, 2012.

Cover Photo used by permission by Dawn Moses, Betts Ministries, www. Betts Ministries.com All rights reserved. November 18, 2013.

Photo Copyright Released from Olan Mills, Lifetouch Portrait Studio, August 13, 2012.

WestBow Press books may be ordered through booksellers or by contacting:

WestBow Press
A Division of Thomas Nelson & Zondervan
1663 Liberty Drive
Bloomington, IN 47403
www.westbowpress.com
1 (866) 928-1240

Because of the dynamic nature of the Internet, any web addresses or links contained in this book may have changed since publication and may no longer be valid. The views expressed in this work are solely those of the author and do not necessarily reflect the views of the publisher, and the publisher hereby disclaims any responsibility for them.

Any people depicted in stock imagery provided by Thinkstock are models, and such images are being used for illustrative purposes only. Certain stock imagery © Thinkstock.

ISBN: 978-1-4908-3156-5 (sc)
ISBN: 978-1-4908-3155-8 (hc)
ISBN: 978-1-4908-3157-2 (e)

Library of Congress Control Number: 2014906603

Printed in the United States of America.

WestBow Press rev. date: 04/22/2014

Contents

Dedicated

to

all those whose hearts have been broken

under the enormous weight of

loss.

God, our Father, says,

Awaken and live again,

for under the mighty wings of Jesus,

our wounded hearts are

healed!

Kenneth and Mary Ann Berry, February 1990

Kenneth Lynn Berry

September 10, 1955–January 25, 2009

Acknowledgments

"Write!" Confidently, this word echoed in my mind. This is what I believe the Lord asked me to do. Even though I did not share His personal direction with numerous individuals, I am incredibly grateful to all the friends and special loved ones who brought encouragement in different forms along the way.

First, thank You, Lord, for continually demonstrating Your incredibly tender love and ever so gently moving me forward by lighting the path You set before me moment by moment. Thank you, Pastors Joe and Connie Voss, for mentoring Ken, for coming alongside him, demonstrating your love and validating him as valuable and precious. Thank you, Larry and Joyce Blanchard, for your faithful prayers, endearing friendship, classic Cadillacs, and challenging mechanical endeavors that Ken dearly loved. Thank you to those at Valley Center Assembly of God church who genuinely befriended Ken and me. Thank you, Dallas Butler and Jim Jarvis, for being there for Ken; your physical strength on those occasions when he slipped out of his chair as well as your friendship are greatly appreciated. Thank you, Brenda and Terry Greenfield; your ingenuity and installing your invention of the ever so helpful "gate" and your friendship has been a blessing. Thank you to all those from Discovery Church of God who made the long trek to CTCA to pray and give personal support during Ken's lengthy and arduous surgery. Thank you to the numerous individuals who presided over and/or attended Ken's two memorial services. Special appreciation goes to Pastor Jim Jarvis, Pastor Terry Cripe, Pastor Bobby Massy, and Pastor Joe Voss and their families. You all are among the sweetest blessings from heaven.

Additionally, I give thanks to our children, who lived through the days with us, loved and have forgiven their dad/stepdad of his shortcomings: Bill Berry and his wife, Suzie; J.J. Berry; Lorissa and her husband, Matt Brunk; Bret Bellina; and Daniel Berry. You are each a treasure sent from heaven and are dearly loved. Also, thank you son, Bill, for moving your family nearby, which enabled you to frequently assist your dad during urgently grave times. Your heart is bigger than all of outdoors.

Thank you, Larry Little, my brother in the Lord, of Apex Flooring in Denison, TX, for reading through my manuscript and lending encouraging words as well as friendship in addition to introducing me to the writings of Andrew Murray. Through them the Lord has planted and renewed His strong foundation of mighty love and strength within me. Thank you, Harriett Nix, for your continued prayers and friendship, as well as editing *Jesus, a Love Like No Other*. Thank you, Cal and Betty Johnson, Kingdom Builders Bible study leaders, as well as all those within this heavenly group. You have given and continue to layer me with, even at the time of this writing, an overflowing abundance of untold blessings. Monique West, your covering of revitalizing thoughtfulness will always be deeply appreciated. Thank you, Jerry B. Lincecum, retired Austin College professor, Telling Our Stories director, and Legacy Writing instructor; you led this writing endeavor as well. Kathy Mertins, dear friend of twenty-eight years and prayer partner warrior, Thank you. To all of the Remnant leaders, each of you have uniquely given blessed and endearing encouragement. Sincerely, thank you.

From the very beginning of this venture, when there were only sixteen pages and I definitely doubted there would actually be a book, before I even knew her name, Lisa Jordan happily and matter-of-factly encouraged me a number of times by saying "Yes, I want a copy of your book when it's finished." Thank you, Lisa.

Suzy and Kenny Kozak, you have been such an encouragement in a multitude of ways. You both are greatly appreciated. Thank you my brother and sisters along with your spouses, Keith and Naomi Hockersmith; Kris Giersch; Brenda and Herb Mattson; and Dixie and Mick Zerr, for your unfailing love, mercy, generosity, and grace.

Thank you to those who prayed and prophetically spoke of the success of an untitled, yet-to-be-developed manuscript: Larry Neilson of Dallas, TX and Pete and Debbie Schneider of Dallas, TX. Thank you, Pastors Raymond England and Brian Ulch, of Trinity Lighthouse Church, Denison, TX and Pastors Bob and Kay Lothenore of the Sherman Church of the Nazarene for reading through the manuscript. You are greatly appreciated for shedding your insight, noting its significance, writing the preface and/or reviews and your encouraging support toward publishing *Jesus, a Love Like No Other.*

Thank you, too, to the numerous unnamed friends and family members who have continued to stay by my side during this journey of bereavement and recovering lost faith.

Last but certainly not least, thank you, my friends, the audience and readers of *Jesus, a Love Like No Other!* May the Lord's ministering angels encamp round about you; may the spirit of the Lord bring you peace and a joy unspeakable, along with the light of His truth, healing, and salvation. And may you recognize for yourself this incredible truth: Jesus is indeed a love like no other.

Foreword

Jesus, a Love Like No Other! is a life-changing, inspirational book that will open your eyes to the love of Jesus. As you will see, it will illustrate the quote "Oh how He loves! Truly, Jesus is a love like no other." No matter how great your struggle might be or how devastated you might feel by the storms of life that have been blowing against your heart, mind, and emotions, Mary Ann's transparent look at her own journey to rebuild her life and emotions helps demonstrate how the power of God's Word and her relationship with Jesus brought her a newfound inspiration, peace, and purpose of hope and life. She captures perfectly how the love of Jesus can change and help us rebuild our lives in time with this quote: "Rebuilding my faith became paramount. Certainly it wasn't instantaneous, but an unfolding progression." Regardless of your place in life right now, I'm confident you, will find this book motivational and inspirational. It is a must-have for *all* libraries.

—Brian Ulch,
Associate Pastor,
Trinity Lighthouse Church, Denison, Texas

Preface

"Get out of the boat! Something big! Something big for you, maybe not for someone else, but for you, it is big!" the woman said as she prayed for my distraught soul seeking to know what plans God had for me now. Ken, my husband of nineteen years, had passed away just a few months earlier. Defiantly, I was not ready to let him go. Surely his life could not have ended; there was more for him. I just knew there was more! But sadly, for us, God took him home.

Sitting in the car after the morning church service, I was overwhelmed with tears and thinking, just how does one "get out of the boat"? Was it more Bible study? More meditation with the Lord? More praying? What? In addition, a commanding thought that somebody had to tell Ken's story played vividly in my mind. After sharing these thoughts with one of my dear sisters, a seed was planted.

"MaryAnn, I believe you are the one," she advised. It, perhaps, was food for thought. Me? I wondered.

Later in the week, a newspaper advertisement jumped out at me. Actually, I had never taken much time to read the daily paper, but on a whim early one spring day I was determined I was going to do just that. This ad expressed a need for volunteer legacy writers with our county hospice organization. Writing a memoir for someone's special loved one seemed especially daunting. Immediately, I turned tail. "No, never could I do that," I told myself. Not only was it too soon after Ken's death, I simply didn't believe myself capable of writing well enough for such a momentous task. And, honestly, my earlier encounter with this organization had left an irrational sense of fear in me. I did not want to deal with anyone or anything that dealt with death. Nevertheless, I prayed that if God wanted me to sign up for these four training sessions, He would keep them heavily on my mind and give me the willingness to take them.

Now, five years later, here are the words written through the intense struggle of countless tears, anguish, and sorrow. In addition, these words are a revelation from within the depths of my heart that I believe God has asked me to share with you.

Albeit now in heaven, Ken has a story, a true story, waiting to be told. You might ask why anyone beyond a family member would even be remotely interested in this account of it. He, after all, was just an ordinary, everyday sort of man.

What might you gain from these few words? Hopefully, you will see the hand of God in your own life as you read through this account of one man's life, which is an illustration of God's mercy and of His love.

Furthermore, seeking His answers to formidable questions continue to unfold. How do you go on living after your loved one leaves this earth? What about the ones left behind enveloped in anguish? A portion of us dies as well. And, what does a person do with a crushed faith? Could this quest for answers be found within the following pages? Could these words be a paradigm of rebuilding dry, broken bones?

I felt the power of the Lord upon me ... Dry bones, hear the word of the Lord ... While I prophesied as I was commanded, there was a noise and a rattling. The bones came together, bone to bone. But there was no breath in them ... So again I prophesied as commanded by the Lord ... And the breath came into them, and they came to life and stood on their feet, a very large army ... This is what the Lord God says: 'My people, I will open your graves and cause you to come up out. Then I will bring you into the land of Israel ... And I will put my Spirit inside you, and you will come to life. Then I will put you in your own land. And, you will know that I, the Lord, have spoken and have done it, says the Lord" (Ezekiel 37 NCV).

❧

Jesus, a Love Like No Other!

Venomously sinister, boiling black clouds loomed menacingly upon the nearby horizon. One could sense they had an existence all their own, like a monstrous, living evil threatening every breathing soul. Surely such a tumultuously wicked sight has never been seen before!

Profoundly etched into my mind's eye, this vision troubled me deeply. What was it, I wondered, some kind of warning? It was February 1990. Kenneth L. Berry and I had been married only a few weeks when the vision came.

I, of course, had learned of his past. Ken had been keenly honest about his life, for the most part anyway. I knew he had been raised as an atheist, that his life from childhood on up had been filled with turbulent difficulties, that he had been and probably enjoyed being the tough, lawless *bad boy*. I knew he had been incarcerated for eight years for refusing to testify against an individual. He said, "It was the code," taught to him by his stepdad, that "you *never* rat out *anyone*." Even though it meant being incarcerated, Ken would not report what he knew to be true about this cohort.

Ours wasn't exactly an ordinary relationship. In fact, Ken was still on parole when we met. At that time, however, I was finally beginning to understand the *Guidepost* article I had read months earlier. It described how through God's forgiveness, grace, and mercy, a lady had married an ex-convict. As she told her story, I carried it for some reason in *my* heart. Bold trust in the Lord is what I thought that lady had. And it had left an indelible impression upon me.

Now, that *bad boy* of days gone by was not the man *I* knew. Jesus had entered into his life and had made him new! The man I had come to know was kind, gentle, humble, loving, and trustworthy. He seemed strong and persistently determined to be successful. Furthermore, he had a deep, quiet inner strength from which he loved the Lord, even though he didn't discuss his faith much beyond saying grace at table. And for a time he met with our pastor as well as with a men's early-morning Bible study group. It just so happened they met around our kitchen table, a table covered with Bibles and dotted with donuts.

I saw him as a *good* man, a painfully honest man too. If asked for his opinion, he would tell his viewpoint without hesitation; stepping on toes was never one of his concerns.

You may be wondering just how we met and what started this whole relationship. Actually, it was a simple phone conversation at our pastor's suggestion.

Aside from my eight-year-old daughter drawing a picture in crayon during a church service and then delivering it to him as a gift, I had only noticed him from a quick glance. He purposely was staying low key. He would stand politely alone, just outside the sanctuary doors after services, waiting for the pastor and the pastor's wife (his chaperones) to finish their usual Sunday morning routines. And, due to being a paroled outsider of both the community and the church, he was being especially respectful and cautious.

At that time I was teaching middle school Chapter I special reading classes and had shared some of my students' rebellious attitudes with our pastor. Evidently the pastor mentioned these attitudes to Ken because he called me during the school day to share a few suggestions for how to guide some of these wayward eighth-grade students.

As he continued to speak, I became keenly aware of Ken's disc-jockey bass voice. That incredible tone definitely caught my attention. What an awesome resonating sound! I thought. I certainly looked forward to meeting him. From deep within my heart I knew that I knew this man and God were about to change my life along with our children's lives forever.

Ken was a man who knew what he wanted and wasted no time getting it. Our lives began to merge as he brought flowers for me and balloons for my children. Before long we were sitting next to each other during church services. His rugged, work-worn, yet soft hands swallowed mine, not just in size, but with an adoring, gentle, tender sacredness and a reverence, like a prayer. Often, he would hold my hand quietly, protectively within his own and up against his heart. Ken's incredible touch spoke volumes to me, more than words alone could ever say about how he loved and treasured me. In addition, since he treated my kiddos tenderly, they liked him too.

Purposefully, with great dependency, I diligently inquired of the Lord asking for His guidance. His sanction for Ken and me to marry was crucial. We counseled with our pastor as well. He was also Ken's mentor, both while Ken was in prison and now in freedom. Our pastor had met Ken during one of his prison outreach ministries and struck up a mutually sincere friendship. Pastor Joe often said Ken was different from most of the other men he counseled; Ken had a tender, sensitive heart.

So, after a whirlwind courtship of three months, our pastor performed our marriage ceremony. I with my two young children, and Ken with his two boys, who lived out of state with their mom and stepdad, became a new family.

Even though the conclusion to the story of that couple in Guidepost remains untold, I really should have known that Ken and I, along with the children, would encounter severe tests. Although I thought I saw life quite clearly through "rose-colored glasses," my vision actually proved to be a bit cloudy. I believed love easily overcomes all; that we'd live happily ever after. We believed that if God sanctioned our marriage, then it would be smooth sailing for the rest of our lives.

Oh no, nothing could have been farther from the truth. What an awakening! Yes, love does overcome; for us, daily challenges were met only through great sacrifice and much prayer. Thankfully, we were committed to each other and to the Lord.

Still unknown to Ken, God had a plan—a bigger plan for his life, a plan to prosper him. God was "making a way in the wilderness and rivers in the desert" (Isaiah 43:19).

Overcoming took place in small increments. Knowing we humans are made up of three parts, the spirit, the soul, and the body, I had been under the impression that the whole person is made new when receiving Christ. Truthfully, it is only the spirit that is reborn, cleansed, and made free from the devastations of sin. The soul (the mind) must learn to renew its thinking by accepting biblical teaching and by spending time with the Lord in study and prayer. The Holy Spirit, our helpmate, teaches us God's word as we study, gives us strength and guidance, and intercedes for us in prayer. Then, being baptized not just in the name of Jesus with water, but also by Jesus with the Holy Spirit and fire gives us the power to be filled with God Himself. The Holy Spirit enables us to fulfill God's plan for our lives (Hebrews 7:25; 9:11–15; 10:18–23; John 1:33; Acts 1:5, 8; Luke 3:16 Holman Christian Standard Bible). In a weakened condition, we may fall. But, through the Holy Spirit, the Lord leads us into the heights of salvation and servant hood, developing a kindred relationship, not rules but a precious fellowship. Thankfully, our salvation is freely given by God's mercy, grace, and love. We need only to ask (Ephesians 2:4–10; John 3:16; Acts 8:15–17).

Unfortunately, Ken had not reached that stage. He had bought into a lie when he was first imprisoned, and it had captured his soul. The lie said he would never amount to anything; he would never again be loved, never again have a family; he would never be wanted or accepted, much less needed. After all, hadn't the chains of his crime claimed his original family and cost him eight years of freedom? Even though God had changed his heart, he didn't exactly see himself as a free man, much less a man filled with God. Furthermore, didn't society not only fear, but look down upon those with a "record"? He truly had lost everything! Right?

Not only had that lie put a stranglehold on him, but Ken genuinely struggled against temptations daily. He told me there was always a slight craving gnawing at him. Do you know that old drug addictions can "haunt" a person forever? It was almost as if the past was demanding to overtake him, to become his future. Could that January vision of black, venomously boiling clouds be the Devil himself saying, "This man's soul belonged to me; now my minions will condemn him unmercifully!"? Or, in retrospect, could it be that the vision was an image of Ken's tormented soul?

Once married, it wasn't long before Ken's peaceful demeanor dropped. Now, as head of the household, he didn't attend church with me and the children very often. His praying became limited to table grace. Past demons were popping up. He didn't want what he perceived as someone telling him what to do, not even the Lord. He seemed angry, temperamental, uncomfortable, searching, and restless.

As an example, when we were returning home from our honeymoon, something didn't set just right to Ken's way of thinking. He stopped the car, jumped out, and angrily declared he was leaving, that I should go home alone and forget about him. He then proceeded to trudge hastily away down the unkempt roadside. Wherever he thought he was going, I surely didn't know, and I'm confident neither did he. Calmly, I asked the Lord for direction. I couldn't just go off and leave him alongside some out-of-state highway. I was unaccustomed to this type of behavior, and it was suddenly starkly obvious that Ken and I were completely opposite with the way we handled stressful situations. Even after surviving a divorce from a thorny marriage five years earlier, I still couldn't relate to Ken's actions.

"Oh God, what do I do now?" I prayed more urgently. Then I just slid over to the driver's side and trailed along behind him, thinking he couldn't have truly meant what he said. Surely it was just some kind of inner frustration talking. I did wonder, though, what oncoming drivers might have been thinking. They would peer at him cautiously as they passed, concern and confusion clearly written across their faces. Thankfully, no one stopped to assist or inquire about our situation.

Again I prayed that Ken would decide to hurry and get back in the car as I was exceedingly uncomfortable with this whole situation. A resolution to it could not come soon enough. Finally, a mile or so later he did have a change of heart. He climbed back into the car and reclaimed the driver's seat. Humbly he questioned, "Why did you stay?"

My reply was simple: he was my husband; I loved him; we were just married; we could work it out; I was his wife, forever and ever; God had plans for us.

Sadly, Ken reacted in a like manner when several other stressful situations overwhelmed him. During these times we received serious prayer support from some extraordinary prayer warriors. Slowly, he began to understand that love does not run away. "Love covers a multitude of sins" (1 Peter 4:8). His trust in me as well as in the Lord was developing.

Obviously, pressure to make good choices in his free life was daunting. Society's rules seemed demanding. Additionally, while he had been away, he had become unaccustomed to family responsibilities. Also, due to parole requirements, he had to maintain employment even if it meant being somewhere with less-than-desirable working conditions.

Full-time employment in a steel foundry was grinding, distasteful, and extremely hard, heavy, dirty work. On the few occasions when he asked me to join him for lunch, he appeared almost unrecognizable. His face and clothing were coated with layers of finely ground black soot. Often, I wondered if his lungs looked the same as his face since he did not wear a protective mask. Thankfully x-rays always proved he had good, healthy lungs, even for one who had also smoked at least a pack of cigarettes a day since the age of twelve.

Although he was especially grateful for his job, he continued to search the ads daily in hopes of finding something better. But desirable employment for a person with his history was almost nonexistent. In addition, his education was another challenge. He had received his GED while in prison and had taken just a couple of online classes offered by a nearby junior college.

I, too, was hoping for a change for two reasons, more out of practicality than anything else—though I suppose a person could almost call it selfishness on my part. First, cleaning his work clothes created serious challenges even for our Maytag. Second, when people are happy with their employment, they are also more apt to be content at home, with life, and with God. I desperately wanted and needed a happy home. Thankfully, the Lord blessed Ken (and me) about a year later with a much cleaner work environment working with machinery in the food industry; even the uniforms were professionally laundered. Wahoo! God did indeed have other plans!

As I look back, I realized it could truly only have been the grace of God that kept us moving forward. Ken had everything against him, except for the love and mercy of God and a lot of love and much forgiveness from his new family.

In spite of what seemed like insurmountable difficulties, Ken successfully sprinkled his new family with moments of genuine kindnesses, love, joy, and caring. My children and I adapted. We learned basically to "walk on eggshells" at times, doing our best to keep a peaceful household. Ken—and honestly, we too—was in the middle of a great transition, somewhat like two mighty rivers peacefully and gently flowing along until joining together, which can create some pretty swift rapids until the union once again smoothes out.

The man God gave me kept me on my knees in prayer. Daily, every single day of our life together, interceding and fighting for my husband the best I knew how was paramount. I told myself this raging war would be won triumphantly. The Devil would not get Ken back, not if God and my faith and prayers had anything to do with it! I sincerely believe in the power of Jesus' intercession and redeeming force. In Christ, we are made new. Yes, there is power in the blood, the Holy Spirit, and in the name of Jesus (Acts 1:8; Phil. 2:10–11, author's paraphrase).

Regardless of Ken's difficult personality, my love for him increased, and many fervent prayers prevailed for nineteen years. Convinced that God had ordained and orchestrated this marriage, this family, we slowly but steadily grew with God's love and grace.

Would you believe that within a year and a half of being released from paying his debt to society, God had blessed Ken with the desires of his heart? Not only did he have a new family with two young children, he also had a decent job, and a new baby boy who truly was the apple of his eye.

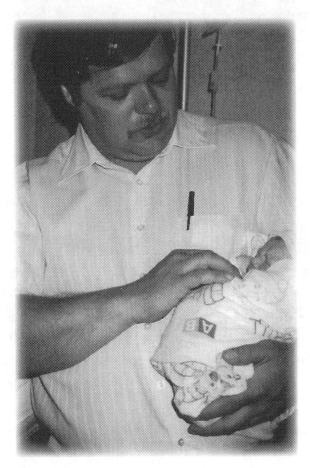

Ken holding his newborn son.

God used this baby as a special adhesive to hold us together when the arrows of battle attempted to separate us. Now, as a family, we had his, her, and *our* children. What is man that God is mindful of him? (Psalm 8:4, author's paraphrase)

In spite of Ken's struggles, he was a generous giver. So, as needs arose among our friends and family, he would graciously and joyfully supply in ways only he could. Discounts from the food processing company where he was employed as a service technician came in handy; a number of church picnics were amply provided with delicious hotdogs. Or, at times, he would lavish thoughtful neighbors, friends, and extended family members with other meats as well. Our freezer was definitely well-stocked, not only with meat but with fresh corn on the cob.

Trekking forty miles to obtain fresh, irresistible, and incredibly delicious sweet corn harvested straight from the field was common during June and July. Ken would purchase several boxes of five dozen ears each, some for our wonderful neighbors and friends, some for us to put in the freezer, and some to have for dinner that very evening and for several meals after. All family members were needed for this event. Young and old alike would sit in lounge chairs under the cool shade of the broad-leafed sycamore trees, hacking off the ends of each ear with a huge butcher knife, shucking, silking, and shooing away flies until all was safely packed away. You would have thought he'd gone to heaven on Earth, his cache being better than gold.

Another example of Ken's generosity was the hefty tips he left, which were greatly appreciated by those who served his table when we dined out or the driver when we ordering pizza. He believed the waiters worked hard for their meager income, much of which was dependent upon customer tips.

Reviewing his life, I see clearly God's hand of blessing upon Ken as well as upon us as a family. This was just the beginning!

Blessings, however, do not always come wrapped up with a bright, cheerful bow. Sometimes they are simply the gift of life!

Just a few short years into our marriage, Ken was diagnosed with a serious life-threatening form of non-Hodgkin lymphoma located in the lower abdominal area.

An urgent phone call from Ken's company nurse said he was doubled over in pain and needed to be transported to a nearby hospital as he had refused being taxied by ambulance. Arriving at the plant within twenty minutes of the call was incredible. My racing rather dangerously down the congested highway could easily have had disastrous consequences! My only thought was, Go fast! Stop lights, yield signs, and passing vehicles were all a blur. I fully understand, now, the importance of trained, calm, cool, and collected ambulance drivers.

Upon my arrival, Ken and the nurse were waiting at the security station. He and I hurried to the hospital. Along the way, Ken, who was leaning forward with both arms wrapped tightly around his middle, quietly but authoritatively instructed: "Slow down.", "Watch that oncoming car.", "I'm okay; you don't have to rush.", and "Look out for that diiiip," as the car's struts begrudgingly performed their duty. His truck-driving experiences, from long ago, led him to never trust a woman driver, or at least that was his excuse for always being the one behind the wheel until this moment. Considering Ken's high level of pain tolerance and all the driving tips he was giving me, I wondered just how severe his pain really was. But then, I thought, perhaps his pain was made more acute simply because I was driving. Or maybe my driving was a diversion from all the discomfort.

What caused this health dilemma? Ken was only in his teens when he was employed as a pest exterminator. Working unprotected with strong pesticides, in the yesterdays before disclosures of chemical dangers to people, was now taking its grand toll. Our prayer was for healing. Psalm 34:7 presents the message, "The Lord encamps round about those who fear Him and rescues them"(HCSB). My interpretation: God was protecting Ken's life as well as our life together. Not only that, but a burning in my soul required Ken to be well; we had a three-year-old son who desperately needed his daddy. Just as importantly, the rest of the family needed him as well. Now, for us, life could only be lived one day at a time with focus on healing.

Aggressively potent and sickening chemotherapy was the required treatment plan. Ken's doctor stated he only had one shot at arresting this cancer. It would be intense! Even though Ken had never been so horribly miserable in his entire life, continuing to work was better than just lying around focusing on the agony. Ken never complained; he seldom voiced his pain or misery. He especially wanted the children—and me too, of course, but especially the children—to live their lives as normally as possible. His comment was, "Complaining would not change a thing." However, we were about to discover the worst was yet to come.

Vigilant quarterly assessments continued only to determine more treatment was necessary. Radiation was the required treatment this time! Day upon day of living with beet-red skin and internally burned soft tissue prevented him from working. Even with his ultrahigh level of pain tolerance, it was excruciating. Yet Ken continued his stoic silence. Seldom if ever did he mention the difficulty of his hardship! While sitting at the kitchen table, he would wittily say after perusing the daily newspaper, "Well, I don't see my name in the obituary; I guess I'm still alive," then give a sheepish grin. However, he wasn't joking! "Swing Low, Sweet Chariot" beautifully and softly whistled by Ken was a proverbial tune of comfort for him during those agonizing days.

This ordeal was way beyond chronic back pain, or having a gash in his ten-year-old hand stitched up by his grandfather, without it being numbed, and in addition to other numerous scrapes and bruises. Thankfully for Ken, donning loose-fitting overalls helped reduce the pressure off his middle, thereby easing a smidgeon of the throbbing—a small blessing.

At one point, he was given a prognosis of less than six months to live. Prayers for healing issued by family members, friends, the church, and especially me, were constant. Ken requested and received half his life insurance payout. Then he liberally gave the kiddos their inheritance appropriate to their ages. Provision for transportation was given to the older three, not new, but good automobiles that would get them to and from school or employment. The younger ones received an exciting shopping splurge that ended with a dirt bike and go-cart. In addition, because debt is like a ball and chain around one's ankle, it was fabulous to have a paid auto title as a result of the insurance money. At the time it seemed the most practical way to support the family.

Due to the prognosis, Ken requested disability from the state but was denied. Evidently, they knew something the doctors didn't. Incredibly, little by little Ken's health gradually started looking up. The tumors continued to shrink and eventually, about ten years later, he was given a clean bill of health. Praise God, for He had another plan!

God continued to honor Ken with new jobs. He was blessed not just with one, but six, each progressively better. He had proven himself to be an excellent, dedicated, and diligent employee.

By the way, he always informed his employers about his felony record. Beyond that, he was extremely selective as to whom he trusted with the information. With fascination, years later, Ken discovered via his brother's sharp eye that his case had been included in True Detective, a magazine detailing infamous felonies. Anyone with an inquiring mind could easily have had access to the details of the reported offenses that sentenced him to eight years in prison. Even though Ken had mentioned the article to me, even handed me the magazine, I for whatever reason didn't read it. The magazine had simply been replaced into its protective envelope and filed away, forgotten. Thankfully, for me, I ran across this magazine article again as I organized important documents, after Ken passed away. Learning the fine points of his crime, though interesting, if it was indeed reported accurately, was certainly a hard knot to swallow.

What love the Lord has for His children! "Therefore, no condemnation now exists for those in Christ Jesus, because the Spirit's law of life in Christ Jesus has set you free ..." (Romans 8:1). The Lord set Ken free from bondage. Amen.

Two jobs that made the greatest change in Ken were based in the medical field. He loved working with the emergency medical services (EMS) and with one of the local hospitals, monitoring outpatient ambulatory care treatment. No two days were ever the same.

Ken's demeanor became softer and gentler especially when working with children. He seemed to be more understanding and relaxed at those times. He even received the Excellence in Caring Award from the hospital management. This position allowed Ken to give back to society; he felt needed and appreciated. And, when any of our kiddos had an urgent injury, Dad was whom they went to, and rightly so.

Interestingly, through Ken's involvement as a volunteer emergency medical technician, he became acutely aware of which medical facilities he preferred treatment at, should the need ever arise. Ironically, he always said, "Never call an ambulance for me. Never." He knew an ambulance call could be rather expensive. He knew the protocol. He knew the people, good people. Additionally, he also knew that as a patient, he would have to submit to the paramedics' decisions. This would be a bit complicated for him as he always endeavored to maintain control of his surroundings.

In one rather humorous account of a call that Ken relayed to us, there was a situation where the person who needed medical help was wearing a down-filled winter coat. Time limitations prevented any thought to the coat; protocol called for promptly cutting it off the patient. Well, adding to the dilemma, feathers went everywhere. One can only imagine what a scene down from the coat lining created in the confines of an ambulance! Getting to the human body for emergency treatment can have its challenges. However, most calls for help were anything but humorous, mostly life-threatening, and some extraordinarily sad.

Personally, I believe the medical field was Ken's calling. He felt he had purpose in it; he helped make a difference. Sadly, though, lack of opportunity prevented him from moving forward in that field. And the choices Ken made earlier in his life were far-reaching.

Family finances being what they were, Ken found work that rewarded him a higher income as a service technician with Harpak to train supervisors and to maintain and repair enormous room-sized, Italian-made packaging machines. This Boston-based company was wonderfully family friendly and caring. Ken, again, felt appreciated and respected. He definitely was an asset to the company. One huge drawback, though: he was out of town a great deal of the time, more than expected.

Being mechanically inclined, Ken was a natural in his position. It seemed he could feel in his being all the mechanical parts and how they worked together. Thus, when a machine went down, he could find and rectify the problem relatively quickly, even when his coworkers were negating his ideas about what was causing the issue. However, at other times searching for the problem could be lengthy and frustrating due to many necessary interviews with numerous in-plant maintenance employs. The indicators and symptoms around the particular machine's disablement had to be uncovered. It could be especially time consuming if the machinery's computerized program had gone awry.

Honey-coating or beating around the bush was not Ken's style with any problem. Often, he was quick to strongly point out human error; down time to him meant thousands of dollars lost in company profits. His determination and perseverance earned him great trust with his employer and the various manufacturing plants, in addition to respect from colleagues.

From his youth, Ken had learned to be a survivor; thus, he had many different manual labor jobs including pest exterminator, shade-tree auto mechanic, long-haul truck driver, welder, filling-station attendant, and even a cook. Being an avid reader, what he didn't know, he taught himself. His strong "can-do" attitude unquestionably contributed to his success.

One tremendous blessing for Ken was when his oldest son, being mechanically inclined much like his dad, was brought onboard with Harpak. For a number of months, they were able to travel and work together while Ken taught him the details of the trade. Of course, son, like dad, had an innate ability to work out the problems the machines were having with apparent ease. Later on, when Ken needed to take disability for the second time, he continued to keep his phone handy. For a time he took field calls from his son and gave suggestions from home, for he had memorized all the machines and knew them like the back of his hand.

And speaking of traveling, travel he did. Even though Harpak had machines all around the world, Canada, Mexico, and the Philippines were his only international destinations. Australia or even Italy would have been awesome, but those assignments never materialized. When he traveled within the continental United States it was normally within the midwestern and southern states, in addition to the beautiful states of Colorado, Idaho, and Pennsylvania.

Ken always showered his family with little souvenirs of love when returning from being out of town for any length of time. T-shirts, sweatshirts, specialty pens, notepads, and knickknacks, most all bearing the name of the place he'd visited created quite a collection for our enjoyment.

Busy, bustling airports were less-than-friendly places for someone carting along a heavy toolbox plus luggage and laptop. Even with the removal of belt, keys, loose change, cell phone, and so forth, without fail he would set off the security alarms. TSA often targeted his toolbox and luggage for closer searches done by hand. Worse, he didn't exactly improve his situation by venting tired and impatient frustrations to the Security officials.

Clearly, I can still see the thoroughly exhausted demeanor he had when I met him at the airport. He could scarcely lift his cumbersome luggage and heavy toolbox into the trunk of our Crown Victoria. At that time, we didn't know just how ill he was or the cause of his gradual decline in strength. He simply forced himself to continue putting one foot in front of the other and believing everything would be better by morning. Generally, he was refreshed by then, for truly there's no place like home.

Beyond his many jobs, Ken's varied interests included a love for reading, animals, fishing, motorcycles, old antique cars, tinkering with motors and, when driving, keeping the "pedal to the metal," and not necessarily in that order.

Our pastor realized Ken's ability to repair vehicles quite early on. Thus, after the old church bus, formerly a tidy thirty-four seater school bus, gave what looked like its "last hurrah," he called upon Ken and a friend for some renovation. Determined to make the old bus run smoothly again, they dug in with sleeves rolled up and high expectations. One quick look caused them to realize they had their work cut out for them. Replacement parts, purchased at cost, as well as travel to distant salvage yards for specific parts no longer manufactured, were all part of the excellence for these two hardworking volunteers.

It has been said that two heads are better than one; perhaps that was the case here, because you could often hear them bantering about how they should best repair the bus while they stood on the front bumper, bent waist-deep into the immense cavity of the engine compartment. Actually, that in and of itself was quite a sight. They deserved praise as well as respect. Being undependable was never again a problem for that rather aged yellow bus when they were finished. And, just as importantly, Ken had made a lifetime friend as well as a wonderful memory. Priceless!

Larry Blanchard (left) and Ken (right) What a team!

Ken would also tell of the times when as a teen he would outrun his small hometown police just for the sheer entertainment of it. Personally, even though Ken would disagree, I think they let him believe he won that "game" and simply called off the pursuit.

One of the officers took a liking to Ken at that time. He recognized Ken's knowledge and ingenuity about the law would be a benefit to law enforcement. Thus, he tried to bring him into the police force. Surely Ken would have had an entirely different life if this prospect could have manifested. With great disappointment to Ken, the powers that be said no, and the opportunity was lost. He had too many incidences of getting into trouble with the law.

Surprisingly, these incidents aside, he didn't receive many traffic violations. Along with his keen, watchful eye, the "fuzz buster" was something of a preventative tool. He intuitively seemed to know where a trooper would be waiting. However, the tickets he did get made up for all the others he should have gotten, especially the one he received while driving through a prevailing construction zone complete with a myriad of earth sculpting equipment and numerous operators. Traffic tickets, it seemed, were somewhat like trophies to Ken. He would call home and off the cuff just mention, "Oh by the way, you need to pay the court," which, of course, fueled a dialog between us about what, where, and why. He already knew what I thought about the situation, so I "bit my tongue" as they say, as there really was no point in giving him a piece of my mind.

As I mentioned earlier, Ken loved fishing. During his middle and high school years, he loved fishing to the point of purposefully getting himself "suspended" just so he could spend three days leisurely catching catfish at a neighborhood pond. Or could it have been his dislike for school rules, assignments, homework, and teachers that made fishing look good? Ken did say once that he really did not like teachers at all -and then he married one. Just the thought alone causes me to smile. God has such a wonderful sense of humor!

His love for fishing triggered the purchase of a timeshare at a beautifully manicured local private lake. After hauling in a pile of luggage and specialty food items, we spent one blessed Thanksgiving weekend in a cute little A-frame cabin at that classy lake.

It just so happened that Ken had just been dismissed from hospital care after accidently slicing off the tip of his thumb in a small industrial accident. Ken displayed the huge, white, corndog-like bandage around his thumb as if it were some magnificent trophy. Instructions for its care included: Do not get wet!

No problem; he believed we could still go canoeing. While still at the shore, Ken climbed into the canoe, showing his family how to do it right. In the process he just kept ... going ... going ... going overboard, and canoe and all flipped over! America's Funniest Home Video's grand prize would surely have been ours if only we could have caught the action on film. Too bad that was before the day of cute little tech-loaded cell phones. Such comedy! We could hardly stop laughing from seeing him drenched, thumb and all, bobbing up, turning the canoe upright, and then finally standing sheepishly waist-deep in lake water. Against my concerns, Dr. Ken pronounced himself and thumb to be "just fine." Damage was limited to his ego. Our little canoe trip continued on and provided lots of unforgettable laughter for days to come. Since there was no fishing on this holiday trip, our fare was just the local grocery's prepackaged Thanksgiving meal-deal dinner.

Other excursions took him and the boys (our sons) Striper fishing to Lake Texoma long before we moved to Texas. Ken's love for this lake and the fishing there became a deciding factor when we choose to move into the area. Bringing home and displaying their scrumptious trophies and acting as valiant providers revealed their need to be adventuresome and "wild at heart." Dinner-table reminiscing of who caught what, how, and when was amusing entertainment for all of us, and, of course, showered us with many delightful memories.

Then there was the deep-sea fishing excursion off Padre Island. Ask any of the boys about witnessing the small octopus being reeled in by another fisherman. It was a fight to the finish! To hear the guys describe the catch, it must have been a truly exciting event. Thankfully, there are pictures, and plenty of them, to document this seemingly wild, tall-tale fish story.

Whether fishing from the bank or from a newly acquired, used boat, it was always a serious undertaking! Ken was not to be interrupted. If anyone had difficulties with their line, or bait, or fish, they learned to handle it on their own, or they merely gave up and took a book to read while enjoying the great outdoors with family. Skewering a perfectly innocent earthworm or immersing one's fingers into stink bait, especially when the catch would only be admired and tossed back, should be dedicated to the devoted.

Of course, there were also those excursions when our little fishy friends benefited greatly from this line-fed banquet. Often at these times, the guys reeled in their catch only to discover empty hooks, which of course frustrated them. Who would have thought fish could display such awesome ingenuity?

Speaking of fish, Ken kept quite a few pets in a forty-gallon fresh water aquarium—none for eating, naturally. Angelfish, neon tetras, gourami, little eels, snails, algae eaters, and translucent shrimp were among his favorites along with the little sharks. Of course, we loved filling this watery habitat with live plants, caves, sunken pirate ships, and bubbly, little scuba divers. Somehow, though, the kids and I managed always to get shanghaied into the cleaning end of things with tank maintenance!

Ken's love for his other pets created a regular menagerie in our house. Perhaps he could have been a great zoologist. However, suggesting he apply for a part-time job at the local state-of-the-art county zoo was greeted with a rather raspy and tart reply, "Scooping elephant dung isn't my idea of excitement."

At one time or another, we were entertained by rabbits, lizards, snakes, tortoises, birds, dogs, and a cat. Other animals such as de-scented skunks, raccoons, sugar gliders, ferrets, and monkeys while desired by Ken, thankfully never made it into the family circle. While these cute exotic critters seem intriguing, surely they're happiest when kept in their own wild environments.

Friends owned and operated an all-too-nearby pet store, and surely it was Ken who kept them in business! Oh, how we (playfully) dreaded the thought of another visit due to anticipating yet another adoption. A kid in a candy store couldn't have had more enticement. Thankfully, he did take to heart my threat of moving out should he come home with a boa constrictor, python, or even a monkey as he insisted he would do. Or maybe he only wanted me to think he was serious. I so often fell prey to Ken's shenanigans. He had a way of teasing where I simply could not tell if he was serious or just kidding.

At any rate, snakes of any size or kind trip an alarm system to my way of thinking, especially ones that could literally squeeze the stuffing out of us. Little ones, I learned to accept—from a distance.

On one occasion, one such pet had vanished from its habitat. During a quick search, I noticed it hiding, being protected behind the tall, old upright piano. Maybe it was silly of me, but even though I knew this thing could not hurt me, I ran outside, grabbed the hoe, and then perched on the piano bench with weapon in hand, just waiting for it to move one little muscle. That was where Ken and the kiddos found me when they returned home. Luckily for that little ten-inch Indonesian garter snake, rescue had arrived. As for me, I frequently made doubly sure that the aquarium lid was securely fastened, always.

Parrots entered our lives while Ken was living through the difficulties of lymphoma radiation treatment. Audrey was the Mexican red-headed Amazon, and Murphy the African Grey. I must admit, they were a riot and great talkers—in English, no less, which still goes beyond comprehension. Honestly, they talked to each other in addition to just talking. Calling what these birds do parroting—just speaking what they hear without understanding it—is truly a misjudgment for these birds.

For example, Ken held Audrey perched on his wrist after giving her a shower. While he used the blow-dryer on the lowest setting to help her stay warm and dry more quickly, this bird excitedly exclaimed, and I kid you not, "Wait a minute, wait a minute, what are you doing?" as she ran up Ken's arm to sit protected on his shoulder near his face. Never would we have believed it if we had not heard it with our own ears. Much later we learned blow-dryers should never be used with birds! Thankfully, she was not injured in any manner.

Audrey managed to be a guest at Bible school one summer evening where she sat confidently on Ken's shoulder. In an outdoor setting, the Jerusalem Marketplace, a living engagement of the biblical era complete with costumes for all participants, became a place where children and adults alike were amazed with this beautiful redheaded bird. However, seemingly becoming comfortable with the setting, Audrey would only say, "Hello," to her admirers at Ken's bidding, nothing more.

Additionally, Audrey was a great friend and company to Ken during his long, arduous days of radiation cancer treatment. They would talk and talk. Audrey, imitating Ken's voice, would call for our little cocker spaniel: "Here Rassie Girl, here Rassie Girl." And little Rassie Girl would dutifully try to find her master until she realized it was just the bird talking. Or, Audrey would say, "Here kitty kitty." The cat being quite unimpressed simply ignored her. Such entertainment!

Sometimes Audrey would call out, "Mmooommm!" with the same intonation as one of the kids shouting from another room. Murphy would raise her voice and respond with the same intonation, "Whhaaaatt? just as if it had been Mom answering back. Murphy also sang along with Ken when he sang, "Bad boys, bad boys, whatcha gonna do when they come for you?" Another antic Murphy enthusiastically participated in was "Hide and seek." Like playing with a young baby, this game would get Murphy to say "Boo!"

Furthermore, both of the birds had gotten so good at impersonating the telephone, we often answered it only to hear a dial tone. Actually, any tone was game for the birds: alarm clock, the microwave ding, the tick-tock of a clock, throat clearing, and any loud or harsh sound, especially intense vocabulary choices whether on TV or in person. Do you know birds love to swear? In fact, we abruptly traded an adult African Grey we acquired through a newspaper ad for an African Grey chick (Murphy), due to its unwillingness to censor its choices in words. Later on, we acquired cute little lovebirds, cockatiels, and even a conure, though not all at the same time; they came sort of one by one. Thankfully, when it was dark, they slept and were quiet for the duration of the night.

Ken's final bird purchase was a rather eccentric Eclectus Parrot, Zoonie. The poor thing picked her chest and back feathers to the point of looking skinned. Ken felt quite sorry for her, so he bought her in that condition from our favorite little pet store where she was awaiting re-adoption. He felt as though he could love her back into being a beautiful pure-red little girl. Evidently there had been too much trauma in her previous care, and she was scared for life. Even though she was one tough bird, sadly she never became the beauty Ken had hoped.

However, this eccentric bird delivered a preciously delicate little surprise just prior to Easter the spring after Ken went to heaven. Talk about being thrilled! Zoonie had been frequently clucking for days while making herself a shredded-paper nest from newspaper lining her cage. Then suddenly it appeared: a very small, white, beautifully perfect prize, an egg. Evidently she received more sunshine this particular season, or maybe her unknown age had something to do with it. I do know we received it as a blessing, a gift, in a sense from Ken as well as from the Lord. Cherished, this tiny egg spoke of freshness, joy, and hope.

One wild species Ken particularly enjoyed watching was sweet little hummingbirds. Their daily summer ritual involved coming boldly to the deck to sip from their feeders and then flitting around the Turk's Cap or petunia flowers, sampling more nectar. These little creatures were amusing to observe. However, as if in continual battle mode, they kept an attentive eye out for any invading competitors. Fearless and determined, they would defend their prized feeding zone by fiercely charging toward any other hummingbirds flying into the vicinity.

On another rare occasion, one of these tiny birds buzzed between Ken and the feeder and then just hovered close by him at eye level. After a minute of this rather strange activity, it dawned on Ken that the bird feeder was empty. He stood up and told the tiny persistent bird to be patient; he would be right back with fresh, sweet nectar. As if understanding, this little iridescent hummingbird waited. Once its tummy was full from the fresh supply, it flew back to Ken, hovered for a second or two as if saying, "Thank you, sweet friend," and then flew away. Even little Rassie Girl enjoyed watching their performance. What a blessing!

Truly, there is no joy quite like the innocence of lying on the floor with puppies. The little cuties crawling, snuggling, licking, sniffing, pulling, nipping, chewing, producing crescendos of giggles from the kiddos remains a favorite memory of ours. These were the offspring of two special canines: Rassie Girl, our sweet little house momma, and the daddy Snickers, who had always been banned to the great outdoors, gave us many adorable cocker spaniel AKC puppies. Parting with them was always difficult, as we were ever so enamored with them. Of course, we loved on them as much as possible those first six weeks while they were still ours.

And then there is Chipper, the final pet purchase by Ken. He's an adorable American Bulldog, distantly related, believe it or not, to Chance from Homeward Bound. He was acquired under great protest as surely we had enough pets. Ken insisted that we would need this dog due to Rassie Girl's aging and poor health as well as his own health issues. One day, he and our youngest son, then sixteen, went on a little visit to a neighbor's home. Sure enough, the one puppy our son had been picked as favorite a couple months prior still needed a good home. Chipper, at the time of this writing, has now grown into a strong, eighty-five-pound, lovable top-dog kind of friend.

American Bulldogs were bred for pulling. So, when grandkiddos came for one wintry visit, it really was not too surprising to see Chipper playfully pulling the youngest through the snow by a coat sleeve. Of course, the torn sleeve on a new coat is another story. Nor was it surprising to discover Chipper could pull three eighteen-year-old boys up the street while they were all on an adult tricycle. In addition, racing and outrunning the go-cart, along with running down any four-legged creature daring to put a paw on his turf, added a bit of comedy to our days. Yes. Pets were definitely an integral part of Ken's life.

Beyond the love for his animals and their antics, attending school events and summer sports with the children were important whenever Ken was home. In fact, one summer, since no one else volunteered, he sincerely attempted to be a flag-football coach for a group of nine-year-old boys, his son included. Given that he had never played the sport, his only knowledge came from what he had watched on ESPN, a cable sports channel. Sadly, and I suppose predictably, the team did not win any of those intramural games. Teaching young boys really wasn't his forte. But from appearances, the boys still had fun trying, even though they were disappointed with the numerous losses.

One quiet activity Ken constantly enjoyed was reading. Be it the daily local newspaper, sports and science magazines, or books, you could find him reading at all hours of the day or night. A lot of this reading material could be found in his suitcase when he was traveling. He also stored books on the bathroom floor, on the back of the commode, alongside his comfortable favorite recliner, and in little cubby holes near his bedside. In addition, the living room wall of shelves was filled with both new and almost antique books. Of course, there would be a couple on the floorboard of his truck as well. True-murder mysteries, history—especially Civil War topics such as Andersonville Prison—Louis L'Amor's Western novels, and Stephen King's horror were among his favorite genres (JHAHN-ruhs) or categories. John Grisham, Robert Whitlow, and Ann Rule were among his favorite authors. He loved literature that created an adrenalin rush and with which he could identify.

Oddly, one book I never witnessed him reading was a Bible, with one exception, even though he had several available. He even kept one under his truck seat. Attempted conversations about biblical ideas or a pastor's sermon usually created tension between us. Religious activity, Christian activities, and discussions had been forbidden during his atheistic childhood, so perhaps that continued to play a role. Or was it just too personal for him to speak about? He would never say. He believed what he believed, and it simply wasn't up for discussion. Ken's endearment to the Word, it seemed, was a private matter.

The one exception was in December, 2008, one month before he left this earth, Christmas Day. Even though Ken's body was swollen, sedated, and rather lethargic in appearance, he read the Christmas Story aloud to his family. He read in a clear strong deep voice, Matthew 1:18-2:12, with his typical intonation, perfectly and uniquely, him. His words, his voice sounded whole, wonderfully normal, and healthy!

You see, while in prison, Ken was accepted into an elite program to benefit special education students. He was trained to read a variety of textbooks aloud. After much practice, his narration was placed on cassette recordings. These recordings were then released to the textbook publishers to be utilized by public and private schools. In turn, children with any type of vision or reading disability benefited greatly when they studied and listened to textbook content via cassette. Participating in this program not only gave Ken a sense of value and worth, but also the opportunity to assist others with legitimate needs.

Making a difference in a struggling life was one of Ken's special desires after he had been set free from the captivity of prison. Participating in a jail ministry was a recurring dream for him. He wanted to give back to society in the same way Seventh Day Adventist visitors and an Assembly of God Pastor had led him to the Lord during his incarceration. Unfortunately, something always stood in the way of him becoming actively involved.

At first, it was too soon after his own release. Prisons vigilantly enforced their standing rules and regulations concerning ex-cons returning to the prison claiming they were there to proselytize. For one thing, Ken had to make an appointment two months in advance. With his impromptu travel schedule, it was impossible to confirm a time this far in advance. Then there were interferences from work hours, illnesses, being out of town, and finally concerns for getting a reputation that might trickle down to the children. Ken always believed he would be able to get involved later on. Sadly, later never came.

I feel impressed, though embarrassed, to respectfully add a bit about a problem we struggled with all of our nineteen years of marriage: our financial accountability. This seems as good a place to insert it as any. Budgeting, at best, was difficult to manage. Please do not look down upon Ken for what I'm about to say, as it follows right along with symptoms of a bipolar disorder. This diagnosis doesn't give license for his actions but is simply a fact.

Ken took great pleasure in buying things. Actually, money in and of itself didn't have much value to him except for the utilization of its power to acquire. Spending it brought him joy. His belief was that he worked hard for it, so he was obliged to enjoy it. I learned quickly to be careful when admiring an item because Ken interpreted that as me hinting for him to purchase it, and he would. Or he would mistakenly believe what we already had wasn't good enough. Giving gifts of meaningful value was one of his methods of demonstrating love for his family.

Ken, to his credit, recognized his weakness for craving spending to the point he would not allow his name to be put on my savings account. He knew he had a hole in his pocket, and if he had access to the funds, he would use them. In addition, separate bank accounts kept us, at least, from arguing over the fundamentals. However, it did not keep him from overdrawing his account or accepting numerous preapproved credit card offers.

When asked about signing up for studying finance and becoming more savvy with these issues, he replied, "I don't need a class in financial management; I know exactly how to spend my money." Even though Ken made buku bucks, there was never enough. Financial security was never ours. Truly, it was not a pretty sight, as I saw him taking us headlong and spiraling downward toward a horrible crash. Of course, my savings were depleted because he knew I would, at least in part, surrender and cover his debt simply out of self-preservation and conviction.

Later in our marriage, he found himself with a gambling addiction. Even though he felt guilty about this activity on one hand, he loved it on the other. I attended an Alcoholics Anonymous meeting once because it dealt with addictions. Our community did not have a Gamblers Anonymous at that time. I knew Ken would never participate, so I went hoping to find avenues of lasting help for him. He had had enough of psychologists and counselors from his days of incarceration, telling him that he needed a change in his thinking to meet society's norms. In addition, one of his dearest friends tried to hold Ken's feet to the fire, challenging him to courageously do the difficult thing by seeking help. Joining an addiction disorder organization, surrendering himself to an accountability group, simply stop going to places of temptation, and dedicating himself to prayer, along with maintaining his church attendance were a few of his suggestions. Unfortunately, Ken continued in that atrocious addiction to the point of lying and attempting to cover up the evidence.

Even though he felt guilty about losing money, he never found the strength to forgo the temptation. All those lonely days of traveling and having too much spare time away from home were filled up with anticipating the golden opportunity of hitting the jackpot. Being faithful to our marriage was not a problem, but abusing our finances was. Occasionally, he did win, intensifying his desire. Excitingly bright, multicolored flashing lights lured him in. Like a bug zapper on a hot summer night to a mosquito, the one-arm bandit was continually beckoning, luring, enticing.

Finally in the later days of his involvement, he asked me to accompany him to witness what all the excitement was about. Surely I would be as mesmerized as he was once I saw the action for myself, he said. Indubitably, I would then understand and happily join him in his carnival of bliss.

Simply, however, I could not. Since I detested the whole demoralizing industry, I wouldn't even attend a concert held on casino property, much less willingly walk on my own volition into this place of what I considered to be death, destruction, and an immense illusion of pleasure.

Even though I loved him dearly, truthfully, I did contemplate separation over this issue. But with much prayer, I realized it would accomplish only one thing: additional anguish. Since the problem would remain, the only decision was to simply love him *for better or for worse*. God could handle it better than anyone else as Ken belonged to the Lord.

Barely a year after moving to Texas, Ken was diagnosed with pancreatic cancer. Once before, Ken had been healed of cancer, so I thought God would surely take care of this as well. Searching for a trusted doctor and treatment center was a bit problematic. Then as suggested by a friend, he explored the Cancer Treatment Center of America in Tulsa and was accepted for treatment. Thankfully, medical insurance would pay for this expensive remedy!

Being at this hospital was such a beautiful blessing and convenience. The doctors, treatments, surgeries, pharmacy, cafeteria, worship services, outings, and outpatient accommodations were there in one huge building.

In our estimation, patients received the most excellent of all possible care and treatment administered with love and compassion. Doctors—among the best worldwide—nurses, and staff members all did everything possible to reduce stress and meet the needs of both patient and family members. We always felt hope, and it was always given.

By the way, with a skilled certified chef, cafeteria food in this hospital was wonderfully delicious in addition to being inexpensive. Patients and their immediate family members received a nice discount on meals, which was extremely helpful for overburdened finances. Dining there was more like being at a relaxing restaurant than a hospital.

Ken's treatment soon began. After managing to get beyond many physical complications and delays, he went through a grueling twelve-hour surgery. One of the renowned surgeons at the Cancer Treatment Center of America in Tulsa was gloriously successful in removing the thoroughly blackened and rubberized pancreas. Once Ken was released from his initial month-long hospital confinement, numerous return visits were required. Ken often stayed three days at a time, receiving his necessary chemo treatments.

On one of these trips late one stormy spring night, a tornado warning was announced not only on the TV weather broadcast we were watching, but also on the hospital emergency announcement system, in addition to staff members knocking on every door to warn us. Urgently, every patient was collected and immediately escorted, with no time to change into street clothes, quickly down into the first-floor interior corridor to sit out the warning as comfortably as was possible. Surely, the patients were mighty in their prayers as well. Thankfully, after an uneventful hour of anxious waiting, we were given the all clear to return to our rooms. This tornado had passed directly overhead, but did not touch down until a number of blocks to the east! Damage was minor. Praise God!

Now Ken's health, though slowly progressive, changed dramatically for the worse. Within a seemingly short number of months came the crushing discovery: cancer cells had metastasized into his spine, causing him to lose the use of his legs. Due to some misunderstandings and medically confusing local situations, diagnosis and treatment came too late to save the nerve impulses. Seven radiation treatments could not reverse the situation. At this point, he had become totally dependent upon me. Still, we believed in a miracle. Nothing was too difficult for God, nothing! He only had to speak the word.

Remodeling parts of the house for handicap accessibility clearly became necessary. We were ever so grateful for our enthusiastic and skilled sons who could build sturdy entrance ramps and enlarge interior doorways, allowing an electric scooter to pass through. (At this point however, I would like to insert a little helpful hint: should you have need of this type of remodeling, do remember to turn the heating and A/C unit off. This will possibly save you hours of cleaning excessive dust off every surface, including the walls, within your entire home!) In addition, a friend devised and installed an amazingly helpful iron-rod device that assisted Ken getting into and out of bed. It had an arm that swung open and stayed in place so Ken could brace and ready himself to sit up as someone lifted his legs and swing his feet onto the floor. From this position he could shift his body onto his motorized scooter and go just about where ever he wanted. Continued independence and freedom of travel, though limited, alleviated his cabin-fever symptoms, and this mobility had numerous benefits for which we were immensely grateful.

All too soon the time came when the frequent three-and-half-hour drive was more than Ken could handle. Due to being easily fatigued as well as being unable to go anywhere without his motorized scooter, he began receiving treatment locally, using the Texoma Area Para transit System (public transportation) bus to get to and from his appointments. The bus would come to our home, and he would board by driving his scooter into the designated, secure wheel-locking spot; I'd meet him at the treatment center.

Before Ken entered facility care, while I was still caring for him at home, I saw a flash of a vision where Ken was quickly walking and climbing up through a cloudy mist. I could see his bare legs quickly and happily moving on their own accord again. Excitedly, I reported it to Ken. He searched my face as if asking whether it could possibly be true. Could he even hope for such a miracle? I confess to you I didn't tell him everything. Being unsure of what the mist meant, I chose to believe it meant healing, a healing that would allow him to be husband, father, grandfather, and friend on this Earth.

Unfortunately, a few medical misunderstandings for care came along after we could no longer travel to the Cancer Treatment Center of America in Tulsa. Or possibly, looking back now, maybe these painful ordeals were orchestrated by the Lord. Perhaps it was all part of His grand plan for Ken's heavenly homecoming. Nevertheless, eventually an open gangrene sore had developed on his tailbone, requiring debridement—in other words, surgical removal. The decision permitting it was excruciating as Ken said he would rather die. While in the ER examining room, he let the whole world know how he felt about the process, loudly cursing it.

One should take a walk in the patient's shoes before condemning here. Ken passionately despised what he knew lay ahead for him; truly, I cannot say that strongly enough. He wanted to be home, and he feared if he surrendered to the debridement, he would never go home again! Full of chagrin and defeat, he did, however, surrender simply for us, to honor his family.

Debridement was horrendously gruesome, and his fears proved true. Even though the surgeon went as deeply as possible, a gouge of four inches long, one and a half inches wide and about that deep could not remove one hundred percent of the minuscule poisonous trails. Talk of trials and tribulations! Ken suffered enormously.

While hoping and waiting for significant healing, he spent the last three months of his life in three different facilities. I had heard an occasional report that he didn't always handle being cooped up and being bed ridden well. However, in every possible waking moment, I was beside him. I needed him to know I loved him. In those times I never heard him complain or saw him get cross, even though he always asked about going home. We hoped, we believed, we prayed, we kept ourselves filled with healing Scriptures, and we depended upon the Lord. Friends had even sent away for a healing cloth from one of the reputable TV ministries. I believed God would heal him. His clothes, including his shoes, were patiently waiting for him to jump into them, walk out of the facility, and go home; the vision of his walking legs was always before us.

"Lord, take us to the other side of Ken's healing," I silently prayed. "We need to be a normal family again. Please." Out of sheer exhaustion from his care, travel, rushing to be by his side constantly, keeping up with employment demands, meeting the needs of our seventeen-year-old son, the stress of insurance hassles, and the futilely of trying to keep up with household chores were taking their toll. I prayed. "Heal him, Lord. Ken needs to come back home." Again, "Take us to the other side of Ken's healing," was my plea.

One Saturday evening, our youngest son had come for a visit alone at my insistence so that he could spend as much one-on-one time as possible with his dad. After a superb time of sharing and just being together, I couldn't help but notice the long, clinging hug Ken gave our son as our son prepared to leave that night. I also noticed the fact that Ken didn't want Chipper to come this time, which was unusual. I could see something in his skin; something had changed. It was not necessarily swollen but tight and rather yellowish, different. He wasn't getting better, and I feared, though I never stated it, that his life now could be in jeopardy. Still, we believed healing would come.

A few days earlier, even after Ken had slumped forward holding his forearm to his chest, and uttering the stark realization, "I'm dying." I couldn't believe his words. Surely, even now, nothing was impossible for God. We—well, maybe it was just me—were not giving up. Ken repeated after me, "I will live like David lived and proclaim what the Lord has done" (Psalm 118:17).

While we watched a televised pastor's dialog on healing the next evening, with Ken in agreement, I called the listed phone number which offered prayer for those in need. Instead of the call going straight to his phone team, I spoke directly with the pastor even while he was involved with his own family member's hospitalization emergency. Kindly, he prayed. But the only words I heard were, "Sometimes an illness is unto death; we don't always know God's plan." No, I thought, it could not be!

Late one Saturday night while preparing to leave for home from the nursing facility, I searched Ken's face and understood he thought he would never see me again. He managed a meager, sincere, woeful smile. Oh, why did I leave? Why had showering, sleeping, and chores been more important? I had always stayed extra late in times past when I sensed a need. But one voice was saying "Stay," and another was reminding me of all the things needing to be done at home.

Early that Sunday morning, January 25, 2009, I was awakened by an impertinent ringing. I answered it, and an urgent voice on the other end stated Ken had been taken to a nearby emergency room. I could no longer deny what was happening. But my heart, in total conflict and anguish, told me the opposite.

En route to the emergency room, I had become impatient and anxious. In addition, our youngest son, who was staying at a friend's house, was not answering his phone, and his friend wasn't answering either. At seventeen, he had a history of sleeping so heavily that only a douse of cold water would rouse him. Still, I tried again. I notified a few other people about what was going on as I drove the fifteen minutes to the hospital.

Ken was having difficulty breathing. Thankfully, though, we could visit a little. He wanted to know what had happened, why he was in the hospital. He was in such a fog. Removing the controversial pain patch and thus reversing its effects brought Ken speedily back to reality. He could speak and think far more clearly. Surely, surely they would find an answer and stave off death, I thought. Questions, questions by the attending ER physician seemed endless.

Friends had arrived, but I still could not get a hold of our youngest son! All the other children were out of town. Events were beginning to become unreal. I was simply moving as directed.

Even though the staff was attending to Ken's needs, it didn't seem to be fast enough or good enough; all was in slow motion. My heart wanted to scream at them; couldn't they hustle? Why the snail's pace! Wasn't this supposed to be an emergency room!

After giving him oxygen and a chest x-ray, a CAT scan was ordered by the ER doctor. I thought it was a good thing, that they would finally learn the best treatment for him. I anxiously waited outside the door while they proceeded with the scan, thinking it was taking too long. I could hear someone calling his name, asking him to cross his arms over his chest and hold them still;

he was not responding. I so ached to rush in. Suddenly, a panic-stricken young nurse flung open the door and quickly beckoned me in. The staff had pulled Ken's cart away from the scanning machine.

He lay there in another world it seemed, trying desperately to catch his breath by taking great gulps of air. In disbelief, as I placed my hand on his shoulder, I encouraged him, "Keep breathing, you can do it, keep breathing!" I wasn't expecting him to stop, not even then.

After one last, huge gulp for air, an enticingly peaceful but quizzical expression filled Ken's face and his eyes as he looked beyond the physical realm. Thankfully, the voice of the Holy Spirit commanded me, *"Look at him!"* Doctors, nurses, it seemed everyone was asking questions, giving information, wanting a decision, needing my attention *now*. But, just for this brief moment, time stood still to be forever remembered, for me to be forever grateful for. It was just Ken, the Lord, and me together while peace, sweet peace was reflected so pervasively in Ken's eyes.

Evidently, God must have said, "Come home." Surely, Ken must have seen a sweet chariot swinging ever so low, accompanied by angels to carry him home into heaven, a favorite song of his.

At 9:45 a.m., furtive, fleeting peace turned into a frantic code-blue call. Ken didn't want to be resuscitated; I knew that. Years earlier, that decision had already been made. But at that particular moment, when the doctor asked what I wanted, to let him go or try to bring him back, without the appropriate legal documents available, I felt free to ask the staff to at least try. Hadn't they just attempted a CAT scan? Surely there was an answer in that procedure. I could tell the doctor didn't think it was the best decision as he asked me if I knew what I was doing. I nodded, but inside, in my heart, I had no idea what I was truly requesting. I was concerned only for the tie of life. Subsequently, we all ran to the ER, nurses and doctor pushing Ken's gurney; there, they shocked his heart, attempting to get a beat. All was to no avail. He had already left us.

Abruptly, hard-hitting pangs of guilt unmercifully criticized me. Lying flat was difficult for breathing; they needed to hurry. But urgency, it seemed, was not sensed by this team. I knew there was no time for waiting to locate an additional tech, so I assisted the team in transferring Ken to the CAT table. Suddenly, it felt as if I had killed him. Thankfully, the instant the thought came to mind, the Holy Spirit spoke authoritatively. "*No, you were trying to help.*" How blessed to have heaven's correction.

⁊ව

Reality was gone; nothing was the same. Hospital routines, guidelines, and friends' consoling words, nothing made sense. What happened to faith? I wondered. Where was God? What about trusting? Death could not have happened! My senses were numb. Yet preparations were looming before me. More phone calls to family were necessary; I still had to reach our youngest son; decisions had to be made. Finding pertinent contact information seemed grueling; we needed assistance from the Red Cross to bring our son in the air force home from Japan and needed our oldest son to arrive from the East Coast and another to come from Oklahoma; our daughter and her husband were traveling in from Colorado; and finally, we were faced with the unbearable: writing an obituary.

"Loving, thoughtful, and ever so generous" describes my beautiful sisters who arrived with my daughter and her husband as well as one of my brother's daughters. It seems as if they must have dropped everything to drive those nine hours to lend their gracious support. Intuitively, they all knew exactly what to do. Just being together in and of itself was most helpful. We cried, worked, made arrangements, even laughed together. What a blessed gift, family! Among the practical gifts of devotion was a simple, short stack of small, yellow legal note pads. The sister who gave me them knew from her own firsthand experience that keeping lists during this stressfully demanding time was crucial for maintaining any sense of order and organization. I consumed every page not only with each day's agenda but also small details I needed to remember.

With greatly appreciated help from family members, together we wrote the obituary. Gratefully, guidance from the funeral home director was available as well. Later, when the newspaper arrived and I turned to the obituary section after glancing through it, one of my sisters heard my first thought. "What's *Ken's* picture doing in here?" My mind was in and out of reality. But we all agreed it was a handsome picture of him.

My tears were few at that point. Pain and anguish were held in the depth of my soul, quietly. My heart said this was *not* true; my brain said it was. But fighting against the truth didn't change the facts or curtail the need to make memorial arrangements in Texas as well as for a service to be held later in Kansas. Ken had always stated he wanted to be cremated with *no* fuss.

I remembered my last view of his body, an empty shell of a six-foot, 185-pound man lying on a stretcher covered up to his chin with a white sheet. His body was now at the mortuary. On that cool January evening, lingering as long as possible, I still felt as though I needed to watch over him, just in case he woke up and needed something. Oh, how difficult it was to leave him there, coldly alone! Among my first burning thoughts after he left us was, "I must go and see whether or not he found his way into heaven." And, now, at the mortuary, it felt as if I was being forced to abandon him. Realistically, it had been seven hours since his last breath. We hadn't left his side. Fisher's funeral home staff had generously and kindly allowed us to be with Ken much longer than usual. They knew our middle son was en route from Oklahoma to say goodbye to his dad. So we had an extra blessing of just waiting. Now, regardless of awkward emotion, time was up. We needed to go home. Refusing to think about what would happen next, I reflected only upon the thought that Ken's ultimate desire of cremation was about to be honored.

When asking the Lord to take us to the other side of Ken's healing, I meant physical healing for more of life on this earth, not death. I had put my very life into Ken from the very beginning of our relationship nineteen years earlier and seriously more so during our last year together. I had been on guard 24/7 for every spiritual attack that might come against our marriage, our family. I had fought continuously for his soul and his life.

Actually, I believe I acted as if I thought I was keeping him alive by my vigilance during the last few months. Most likely there were those who believed I was a bit off my rocker. Acknowledging this defeat was an extremely bitter pill to swallow. Not only had God failed, but I had as well. Although I was driven to do all that could be done, it wasn't enough. The truth is, my wisdom and faith in healing fell short. Now I held both as worthless.

Everyone at Fishers Mortuary in Denison, Texas, had been extremely gracious, kind, and loving. I could not possibly have asked anything more of them. With greatest respect and kindness, they cared sincerely for all the details of our needs.

A friend took a couple of pictures of Ken and me after he had expired. As shocking and repulsive as it is, these pictures, especially the close up-one on taken with my cell phone of just Ken, presented authentic and absolute truth to me. Patiently over and over again throughout the next arduous months, the pictures, like a bolt from out of the blue, stunned me, proving once again that Ken was not just away on a business trip. He was not returning. He was, in fact, most truly dead, alive only in heaven.

Miracles? I thought. Where was the anticipated healing? But maybe, maybe the miracle God gave us was extended time; Ken lived twenty-two months after the diagnosis, which is considerably longer than average. Maybe the miracle for our family was that Ken took any treatment at all. He did all of it just for us; the pain he endured was for us as we were unwilling to just let him go. He had been down this agonizing road once before and had said "Never again."

Looking back, maybe the miracle was that he didn't leave us on his fifty-third birthday five months earlier. When upon arriving home from school on that day, I found him lying on his bed and in a diabetic coma with a rather gray skin tone. Definitely, he appeared less than alive.

The message I'd heard earlier while still at school seemed true then. As I was leaving the school parking lot, rehearsing the usual after-school routine of exercise, running other quick errands, then heading home for a small birthday celebration, a soft, matter-of fact-statement played in my mind: "Ken is dying today." Thinking I was just imagining things, I almost ignored the message. Instead, thankfully, I rushed home, wondering, "What if ...?"

When I found him, he hadn't moved, not even a smidgeon from his initial morning routine. That morning he stated he was feeling tired, and even though he was fully dressed, he was going to nap before starting his day. For one taking an oral chemo treatment, and after the rigors of being dressed, this didn't seem out of the ordinary. And two visitors were scheduled to attend to him during the day, so I didn't think twice about it. Ironically, his visitors didn't come. In addition, Ken wore an insulin pump programmed to deliver a specific amount based on regular meal times.

While en route home, I called ahead and asked our youngest to check on his dad. Even after shaking him to no avail and then clanging metal cooking lids together like a set of cymbals, Ken didn't even flench. Checking his blood-sugar level upon my immediate arrival home proved it was far too low. In addition, after we took him to the hospital, it was noted by the ER nurse that his oxygen was also at a level far too low.

When the ordeal was over, Ken was a bit upset that we had called an ambulance for life care; he said we should have let him go. Now I ask you, just how does one do that? Just let him go! Where there is life, there is hope! Right?

Another miracle came to Ken and to us as a family in the form of forgiveness during the latter days of his struggling with health issues. A couple of the children chose love to cover some rough times, some long ago difficulties, in their relationship with their stepdad. Naturally, children and their parents do not always see eye-to-eye. But, with a stepparent, disagreements and misunderstandings seem more emotionally alienating. Perhaps this is due to an intensely fragile bond of love. Thus, their forgiveness brought a wonderful wave of peace, both to themselves and to Ken. What a miraculous gift!

A lingering question: why did God take him to heaven instead of healing him here on this earth? Ken was only fifty-three years old. Surely his race wasn't finished (Hebrews 12:1b).

For Ken and I, was our marriage picture-perfect? No. Were there struggles? Yes. Did we do everything just right? No, absolutely no! But, most importantly, was God glorified in this marriage? Yes, most definitely, yes! Would I do it over again? Absolutely, in a heartbeat, especially with the wisdom of yesteryears! In fact, I told the Lord just a few days after Ken left that I wanted to do it all over again, only this time we would love better.

What would I do differently? The first thing I would do differently would be to insist on Ken seeking out necessary medication or treatment to prevent the detrimental effects of depression. He could have had a warmer relationship with God, with me, and with the children. He wouldn't have had to struggle as much if he would have surrendered to medical intervention. Another thing I would do differently would be to smother my husband with more love, more of what he would recognize in his personal love language.

Day-to-day living blinded us to the unfolding of major miracles. Nevertheless, God restored what the locust had eaten (Joel 2:25, author's paraphrase), and I'm reminded of the Scripture, "What is the son of man that You look after him?"(Psalm 8:4). What a glorious love God has for his people! He's just waiting to lavish us with His blessings. We simply need to stop struggling and allow the Lord to cleanse us, to heal our woundedness, to strengthen us, and to abide in us. Life, following the word as the lamp unto our feet and a light onto our path (Psalm 119:105, author's paraphrase) is far more rewarding than demanding our own way. When I consider how God orchestrated Ken's life, brought him the desires of his heart, and loved him, it is more than I can contain.

Today, according to the Lord, Kenneth L. Berry is walking and talking and telling Him, the Great I Am, He is his own!

Ken's cheery wave of "see you later."

What now? It was the question of the hour.

Many unresolved issues needed answers. Initially, my thoughts were based on self. I was feeling hopeless from an overabundance of adjustments I had to make.

Eventually, I admitted that Ken had been right about Chipper. We did need him in more ways than one. It seems strange that a pet could help bridge the gap between life and death. Chipper was the transition because he was the one living thing we all had shared and loved.

Our youngest son needed him to help smooth some rough times during the last months of his high school senior year. Then, after he left for college in Wyoming, I needed Chipper. Anyone who came to the house backed away when they heard his resounding bark and the force of hitting the door with all four paws to fiercely announce arriving visitors. He had become quite the protector and my friend. Ken's response, if he knew, would probably be just a quiet, knowing nod plus that *I told you so* grin.

Texas; why Texas, far from family members? We had lived here for only two and a half years, much of which was filled with Ken's health issues. Even our youngest child had left for tech school, which was more than a seventeen-hour drive away. And how was he handling fatherlessness? He wasn't talking about it. Could I have put a huge spiritual stumbling block in our youngest son's life because I was so confident his daddy would live? Even now, five years later, when talking about the promises of God with him, he seems to have a silent "Yeah, right!" attitude as he walks away.

Our mind-set was on living, thus he trusted my words, fully expecting his dad to be well. Our youngest son would have spent more quality time with Ken if he had been prepared for his death. What about the other children? After Ken's death, everyone seemed estranged, quiet, and faraway. Surely, each child was grieving in his or her own way.

Standing in the driveway each day and each evening, looking up and searching through the atmosphere and hoping for a glimpse of heaven was futile. Nevertheless, I longed to see heaven, literally. Ken was there, and I needed to stay connected to him. Never was I this anxious when my grandparents, older sister, mom, or dad passed away. For them, it was a natural progression and an expected outcome. Of course, I had grieved their absences, but much differently.

A false tunnel vision of sorts developed, as if I was wearing blinders. Nothing was actually wrong with my eyes, but they were not seeing. Looking at people eye-to-eye was impossible. Remembering, trying to describe a new person could only be accomplished in a vague sort of way; details were illusive. This illusiveness carried into other areas of my life too. Stopping at a traffic sign was something I could do, but only by the grace of God did I narrowly escape a couple of accidents due to not seeing oncoming traffic. I was seriously adrift in another world.

How could my children and I find our way? Truly, I did not know the answer. There is *no* map in this giant, arid wilderness. Life now was devoid of meaning. Why was it that God did not heal Ken? The question remained. We had trusted; we had believed. We had followed the Bible's direction: go to the elders of the church, let them anoint you with oil so that you might live (James 5:14–16, author's paraphrase).

We had sojourned the eleven-hour round-trip for that single purpose. We went for the anointing oil and for serious prayer. Meeting at a dear friend's home, trusted, devout prayer warriors and friends gathered to pray over, with, and for Ken. He was filled with the presence of the Lord, totally surrendered. Yet, things didn't happen as we had anticipated. Why not?

Another seriously gripping question hung in the air: just exactly what does a person do with crushed faith, dashed hope, and confidence lost? As far as God went, was He even listening? Surely not, it seemed. Did He even care? Did He actually have a plan? What was the plan? What was the meaning of life? What was I supposed to do? How was I to know? Who was I now in all this desolation? Where was God in all this upheaval? Was it even possible to reconnect with faith? Had we believed in vain? Were the teachings from our pastors wrong? Who were we to discuss these pertinent questions with? Who could I trust to give me solid truth?

In addition, sweet and kind, well-meaning friends along with concerned family members started asking questions. What was I going to do? Then they suggested I move home to be near them. Being wanted and receiving their suggestions were wonderful, but decisions! Questions! Oh so many questions and no satisfactory answers. Nothing seemed right. My mind could only function on remote control. My thoughts were in a constant and horrible whirl; they would not settle. It seemed I could not think even one complete thought without other disruptive words and questions forcing their way into my mind. What could possibly mend this gaping, imploded heart and soul?

In the midst of all this uncertainty, there was one guarantee: paperwork! Oh my, papers were stacked in neat little piles covering the dining table, each a category of its own. And it stayed that way for months. I couldn't move or put these important documents away for fear they would vanish in the chasm of overstuffed file drawers or other "safe places."

Even though Ken had the foresight to have a will drawn up, many additional legal forms needed to be updated. Ownership of property, the house, and the car; life insurance beneficiaries; the name on various utilities making me the primary responsible person; and the list goes on. Additionally, most changes required a copy of Ken's death certificate, which presented a predicament a number of months later.

And what were these forms asking from me? Some forms stated: Choose one: Married____, Single____, Widow____. My mind could not wrap around that one word, *widow*. Remorse filled me when thinking about it. Not only that, but I felt as if I would suffocate as it so powerfully accentuated *death*. Was I still a Mrs.? Was I a Ms. or a Miss? Truly, I didn't know.

While in the financial department of my school district's central office, I needed to make this obvious selection. But tearfully, I didn't know how to answer. Again, I truthfully didn't know what I was anymore. Comfort followed as the secretary so sweetly and compassionately answered for me: "Misses" (widow was not one of the options on their paperwork). Emotionally and mentally I was definitely still married.

Suffering through the loss of a relationship is like being sacrificed under the pestle in a mortar dish, being thoroughly ground up and pulverized into a dreadfully ugly mush, then left to dry in unbearable heat, alone, quickly becoming nothing but powdery dust, completely unrecognizable from what you once were. It is relentless agony in which one suffers tremendously. And becoming utterly *nothing*, just a finely ground powdery substance desiring only to blow away into oblivion at the slightest provocation was torture. Who could shield me from this extreme? Who could survive it for me? Who could put me and our children who were so far away back together again? Why this road of seemingly complete solitude?

Undeniably, living through all the various coinciding stages of bereavement presented challenges. Grieving has various multifaceted physical, emotional, and even spiritual levels. Some professionals say there are seven stages in this rather lengthy process. Rebelling against these disconcerting labels, as if some mechanical or predictive force could put an end to the profoundly deep pain, came naturally to me. Events in life are disjointed. During this traumatic time, the mind can go off on disordered tangents. There is no rhyme, reason, or sequencing. It's a bit like bumper cars. You remember bumper cars from the amusement park? Grief is like a similar, though rather surreal version of this. It's everyone for him or herself, and getting from point A to point B is crammed with jostling and frustrating challenges. You think you can beeline it to your targeted destination only to abruptly suffer whiplash as your car and body are violently rammed into, causing a dizzying, sudden change in direction, or maybe even becoming hopelessly trapped and surrounded by further obstructions.

Unlike Ken and the kiddos—well, the boys anyway—who loved this amusement-park ride to the point you could barely get them off it, I felt as if I had been run over by a Mack Truck whenever I went on it. Ugh! So I participated by cheering them on from the sidelines. Now, at this moment in life, it seems as if I was in both places simultaneously, surrounded by obstacles in motion as well as observing all the action as a bystander.

Because the earth still revolves, and life continues on its way, the grieving person is left not only to deal with the usual daily events, but also to fight for sanity. The mind seems to be out of commission. *Nothing* is the same any longer. That one person with whom you have built a life together as one is now gone, permanently.

Another analogy I've found useful is that one's heart, mind, arms, and hands feel as if they've been crudely and horrifically amputated. Nerve endings say that body part is still in place. However, attempted use sends you recoiling in pain. You search for the member. Time and again you continue to be shocked; it's totally absent, eternally gone.

During this process of grieving, more questions came. I confess, as I mentioned earlier, that confidence in my God was wiped out. Even months after Ken's death, it felt as if He had packed His bags and left right along with my husband. Of course, I remembered what I had believed and had been taught. Of course, I still believed in God as sovereign, but it was strange. My boat rocked violently, threw me overboard, sank, and left me barely treading water, exhausted, and about to go under. Surely it was useless to pray, I thought. God wasn't listening anyway, was He? *He* ignored our prayers. *He* let Ken die! *He* put me in this unappreciated "wilderness." Suddenly, Abraham's journey—or better, the Israelites' journey—seemed to be my destiny as well: an untamed and parched wilderness. Why? I wondered. What to do? How to do it? What to believe? Where to go? How to get there? Whom to trust? Whom to follow? Again, why? Now, not why did Ken die, but what was wrong with our faith, my faith? My lament continued. Why were the Scripture verses void of healing? Ken died. God had not healed him on this earth. Had we put our confidence in deception and error?

Still, from the spirit of God rooted deeply within, I knew one thing with clarity: God does not make mistakes; therefore, this misery could not be His fault. Obviously there must be an enormous error in my belief system.

Silently, time does move on. More or less, I was wrapped in an invisible isolation. Even though one looks the same from the outside, eats and sleeps, goes to work, talks, hears, makes small decisions, and might even smile or chuckle a bit, *nothing* is normal. In fact, this experience cannot even be truly identified with or truly understood until *you* go through it yourself. And I'm confident it's different for each individual. In addition, at the same time, it seemed to me society expected this grieving person— me—to *get over it*! To move on within a month. Forget him.

Simply put, my friends, it just does not happen like that. One must gather strength and courage and rebuild one's life. And this can take an enormous amount of time, not to mention effort. Ken's life was valuable, not something to ignore or put away on the closet shelf.

A few days after Ken's death when I was still numb from shock, a foreboding blackness began creeping up and rotating across and around the circle of my mind's eye. A blackness so deep and dark nothing else could be seen. Willingly, oh so willingly, I began to fall into that sea of utter darkness. It seemed wonderfully and enticingly good to just disappear, leave behind the isolation, endless questions, numbness, and emotional anguish. When this present darkness had covered about three quarters of the circle of my mind, a commanding, authoritative voice, loudly and from within, shouted, "No!"

Instantly, the blackness vanished, leaving me wondering, "What just happened What was that ... that absolute blackness?" Obviously, it wasn't good. Was it despair, irreversible depression, severe mental illness, the pit of hell, or just nothingness? I didn't know.

And, wow! How wonderful to be cared for by the Holy Spirit. Surely only God's grace protected me. Even though I was incredibly grateful for this demonstration of love coming from within my spirit, I was actually disappointed. I truly wanted that fluid relief of drifting into the darkness, even if it was a deceptive ploy. Seriously, what an awesome God to care for me during such despondency! In retrospect, surely, that is one enormous miracle.

Holding on to Ken was consuming me as I unquestionably was still not ready to let him go. I had a ring made that I paid for in part from the cash remaining in his wallet: a simple but expensive dark-blue sapphire heart-shaped stone, our birthstone, along with the diamond chips from his wedding band were arranged on the band as if being held by hands. An odd feeling inside told me I should not do this; I did it anyway. I also felt I should not wear the ring; I wore it proudly. Hungry soul ties between Ken's soul and mine, gripped on to me from deep within my spirit. Each time I studied the ring, I could see Ken's face, his eyes, his last smile reflecting from the stone. It was immensely unnerving. But, for a number of months, I wore it. I held Ken wrapped around my finger; I kept him as close as I could keep him.

It would be several more months before I returned to attending church services. So I wore the ring until a visiting evangelist from Florida, Billy Burke, spoke at church about breaking unhealthy soul ties. Jewelry and pictures are the number-one items that tie us to another individual, he said. In our distressed and torn emotional state, it allows dangerous familiar spirits to enter into our spiritual realm.

After careful consideration, prayer, and wanting to be obedient to the Lord, I laid the ring aside. Removing it was difficult at best, yet I knew from within that if I was ever to be emotionally and mentally healthy, I had to put this dependency away. A few months later, my wedding ring joined the sapphire heart.

During these months, a friend of Ken's had a need for a laptop computer. Ken's was actually of no use to me, so I thought I'd sell it along with all the paraphernalia, such as the computer bag, miniature printer, wireless modem, and so forth. As the friend was examining the laptop and we were making the sale, I heard in Ken's voice explicitly command, "Do not give my computer to him."

Whoa! My first thoughts were, "I'm not giving it; I'm selling it. Surely that's different." The transaction continued. Afterward, consuming guilt and superstitions plagued me. I knew Ken could be rather possessive of his treasures. Even though I do not believe he could see or hear anything going on here on this earth, there was only one thing for me to do: ask for the machine back. When I did, the taunting ceased. It's just a machine. I don't have an emotional tie to it. But now it sits unused and wasted.

I understand now that familiar spirits know us pretty well. They lurk in the emptiness of our mind especially during traumatic times. They can imitate the voice of the one we loved. They want control. They will haunt and roam through the mind if allowed. They are deception. They are evil.

So, in the name, authority, and through the blood of Jesus, I commanded that spirit to go back to the seat of its assignment. It had no choice. "So that at the name of Jesus every knee will bow of those who are in heaven and on earth and under the earth—and every tongue should confess that Jesus Christ is LORD to the glory of God the Father" (Philippians 2:10–11).

I'm so thankful for godly teaching from strong, knowledgeable, spirit-filled pastors! "For lack of knowledge, my people are destroyed" (Hosea 4:6). Yet, if in the name of Jesus these spirits had to leave, then I wondered why Ken's disease did not heal.

Another healthier means of being close to Ken came through searching his Bible page by page. I was hoping to find some secret, a message from his heart, anything to hang on to forever. One Bible, the New Century Version, had been purchased by Ken just a couple of months before he lost the use of his legs. Even though it was important to him, I had never witnessed him reading it. Surprised and eternally grateful, I found a few underscored verses. What does a man living the last days of his life find important enough to highlight? Reading these Scriptures was like looking directly into his heart of hearts.

"Then anyone who calls on the Lord will be saved" (Acts 2:21NCV).

"Why are the nations so angry? Why are the people making useless plans? The kings of the earth prepare to fight, and their leaders make

plans together against the Lord and his Christ"
(Acts 4:25–26 and Psalm 2:1–2 NCV).

"These people made your plan happen
because of your power and your will. And now,
Lord, listen to their threats. Lord, help us, your
servants, to speak your word without fear. Show
us your power to heal. Give proofs and make
miracles happen by the power of Jesus, your holy
servant. After they had prayed, the place where
they were meeting was shaken. They were all
filled with the Holy Spirit, and they spoke God's
word without fear" (Acts 4:28–31 NCV).

"We know that in everything God works
for the good of those who love him. They are
the people he called because that was his plan"
(Romans 8:28 NCV).

"I am not ashamed of the Good News,
because it is the power God uses to save everyone
who believes—to save the Jews first, and then to
save non-Jews" (Romans 1:16 NCV).

"Don't become angry quickly, because getting
angry is foolish" (Ecclesiastes 7:9 NCV).

"When life is good, enjoy it. But when life is
hard, remember: God gives good times and hard
times. No one knows what tomorrow will bring"
(Ecclesiastes 7:14 NCV).

"You know that many times you have insulted
others" (Ecclesiastes 7:22 NCV).

"I learned that it is foolish to be evil, and it is crazy to act like a fool" (Ecclesiastes 7:25 NCV).

"I have seen real misery here on earth: Money saved is a curse to its owners. They lose it all in a bad deal and have nothing to give to their children. People come into this world with nothing, and when they die they leave with nothing. In spite of all their hard work, they leave just as they came" (Ecclesiastes 5:13 NCV).

Awesome truth. What a precious gift!

꿈ᐒ

Group grief counseling was suggested by family members. Stubbornly, wanting to hold on to my grief, I refused to go. I couldn't bear to hear the burdens of others; I was far too consumed with my own. However, I gladly consumed several books and pamphlets concerned friends and relatives sent me. Surprisingly, I found myself in those pages, in those words, and thinking, "How did they know? Exactly, that's exactly how I feel. It seems odd that others could have felt the same as I did."

A dear friend suggested journaling my thoughts, memories, messages I'd like to share with Ken, or just things that happened in my daily life. The idea was for me to just take things one moment at a time, write about them, and absorb one day's thoughts one at a time. Amazingly, this idea began to work wonders once I actually started.

Writing required—for me anyway—a beautiful journal, not just any old spiral notebook, even though paper is paper and would have held my words just as easily. Today, an Amazing Grace Journal holds and treasures my words, my pain, my thoughts of Ken, and has them bound forever in its own beauty, which miraculously ushered healing into the depths of my soul. Eventually, seeing and reading my own thoughts seemed to assist in a much-needed reordering of my thinking processes.

Thankfully, I had a wonderful position as an elementary school library aide. I greatly loved this assignment. Now, as far as employment went, truthfully, I hated going to work after Ken's death. I wanted to go away; I wanted to be totally alone. Two weeks off for bereavement is not near enough. But, in reality, I needed an income. I felt caught between a rock and a hard spot, living in two different worlds. Dutifully, like a wounded wooden soldier, I made the tearful trip to and from school each day, forcing myself to stop the tears, to redo my makeup before exiting the car, to smile, and to think of the students' needs ... after all, the elementary-school-aged children would be upset if they saw their librarian distraught.

Actually, after a season I could see these children were in a sense, a lifeline. Their tender and sincere little hearts displayed God's love through their hugs, handcrafted cards, and sweet smiles. They were full of sympathy, and I would see most of the children daily. My colleagues were incredibly and equally supportive. Never did I lack for anything, not really.

Catching me totally off guard, there were a few times when tears just flowed, while reading a story to the students. My heart would ache from a sudden flashback of emotion and new empathy for the main character's plight, and, of course, it caused a demonstration of tears. Concern from the students was evident as well as from the visiting teacher. However, simple explanations of my seemingly out-of-place weeping would put them at ease and give them understanding. Additionally, it essentially taught the students an important reading-comprehension technique: that of identifying with the character.

After a few weeks, one of our custodians mentioned that I must be a good actress or very strong; that was hardly so on either count. My mind-set during the day had settled on allowing me to partially believe Ken was simply away on business. But, when faced with going home after school, truth severely gripped me. I didn't want to go home. Finding many new alternate routes and lengthy, winding roads eventually led me tearfully toward home and helped prepare me for the hollow emptiness I'd find there. Once it was a home; now it was only four walls, and felt as if it were foreign territory.

Yet, oh, how I ached to be alone... alone... alone. I wanted to grieve. Everything in me yearned to grieve. But grieving had to wait. It had to wait for an available time, like holidays, weekends, and summer break. Climbing up and standing on the rooftop and simply bellowing out groans of anguish until no sound remained could have been extremely therapeutic. Of course, that didn't happen. Instead, I waited.

And speaking of time and additional complications, it was nearing the end of March when I felt it important to file our income taxes immediately. So after making an appointment and gathering all the pertinent information, the accountant quickly completed the task. Then I received word that I would have to mail the forms instead of filing electronically. After not receiving my refund, I asked our preparer what was happening. Finally, the IRS informed me they had already deposited my refund and gave the banking details. They did not match those of my financial institution or the information I had filed. Identity theft had reaped someone a huge sum of money all in Ken's name one week before our tax report had been filed.

Following hours of phone calls and speaking with numerous people, an investigation was launched. I had to prove I was the rightful owner to a refund. My heart was at peace during this ongoing situation, as I felt as if everything would eventually work out. The major question was: who had access to Ken's social security number? The answer: personnel in every business office who said they needed a copy of his death certificate. Eight months later, with interest, I received my rightful refund. My advice to others in this situation is to notify the IRS and all credit-reporting agencies immediately after a loved one passes away. Ask them to flag the deceased's Social Security Number. Since this time, I have learned the deceased are the most common victims of identity theft.

Another helpful tip regarding finances is to leave your spouse's name on your financial accounts, such as checking and savings accounts. Years later, out of the blue, funds may arrive from a rebate or overpayment generated from a previous credit card or some other account. Likewise, depositing a check written to the order of your spouse will be easier if his or her name remains on the account.

In the midst of these troubling times, my daughter, a family counselor by profession, suggested that I become more involved with things that gave life, like planting trees and flowers—whatever would create life and beauty. She never presupposed my emotions, never told me how I was to feel, nor did she even attempt to be my "psychologist" or push her ideals on me. She simply shared comfort and love even through her own grieving.

So when early spring finally arrived, I liked the idea of planting life. It was time to dig up the soil. Once out in the spring weather, I realized I needed and loved being in the sunshine. It became a rejuvenating essential. I started by planting, with a little assistance, a beautiful Oklahoma Redbud tree, a species Ken and I had considered planting the season before. Eventually it would shade the hot deck perfectly in summer. Doing that led to planting flowers like rose bushes and something that looks like holly, but grows clusters of grape-like green berries, a fascinating plant. Interestingly, everything I planted, aside from the tree, had thorns as well as beautiful flowers—the beauty along with the pain in life, I suppose.

Surely only projects worthy of painful blisters and broken and grimy fingernails could bring healing to the soul. I began to feel a bit of that restorative life again. Something from the sweetness of life, new life from the Lord, had been planted within me as well. It was a seed.

Furthermore, three months had passed since Ken's death. I was now attempting to force my brain into thinking more clearly, so I enrolled in a children's literature class that required three lessons with students along with a summative essay. The student lessons would require documentation proving that elementary students had actually been involved. All assignments would be due within five months. Surely that would be more than enough preparation time. Participating in this class along with two hundred other educators rescued me from familiar surroundings as well as dwelling on Ken's absence.

The instructor, being a knowledgeable popular speaker, demonstrated a plethora of ideas about how each story would benefit our elementary students. She recommended numerous titles all from current fiction and nonfiction library books, often referred to as "trade books". Even though I still felt numb and a bit like a fish out of water, I truly liked being in this familiar educational setting. It felt wonderful. And, because the class offered a portion of the credit I needed for renewing my teaching license, I was utterly determined to make it work. It was a huge challenge. After the one-day seminar, the remaining assignments would be completed a little at a time and only through God's grace.

The summer sun brought plenty of opportunities to be physically active in the great outdoors. Yard care and mowing almost two acres of property was now my responsibility and became my number-one venture. Basking in the sunshine from the seat of a lawn mower was indeed a breezy, bumpy ride but felt awesome. Sunshine and fresh air began replacing the entangled cobwebs of my mind with a spirit of peace; yes, there was a tidbit of tranquility. I could hardly believe it, another small stepping-stone. Realizing that the joy of the Lord is my strength caused me to also remember, "I am able to do all things through Him who strengthens me" (Philippians 4:13).Thus, if God says, "I am able," then I am definitely able.

On one such summer day about seven months after Ken's death while I was out mowing, songs from the long-ago past came to mind, wonderful, sweet choruses that usher in the presence of

God—the ones from the late 1980s. While they soothed parts of my crumpled soul, it dawned on me that those songs, while gloriously beautiful, were never going to return to the popularity they once enjoyed. Their season of grandeur had come and gone, like Ken, forever. Agonizing reality finally hit me: he wasn't just away on a business trip; he was not ever coming back. I would never see him on this earth again!

By now, nine months had passed since I last attended church. An urgent longing had developed in me for Christian fellowship. Being part of a women's assembly seemed especially important. I knew I needed help. I needed to allow the Lord to be alive within me, but where to go? How was this to be accomplished? Because I was still buried under what felt like insurmountable mental heaviness, the process of thinking was complicated. In fact, I didn't even want to think. How did I get by? Surely, the Lord quietly carried me moment by moment and silently into the next day.

$\mathcal{S}$

Rebuilding my faith became paramount. Certainly it wasn't instantaneous, but an unfolding progression. "In the beginning God created…" (Genesis 1:1) seemed the best place to start building. Reading God's word did begin to bring a sense of renewed spiritual peace to me. My new purpose was to read Scripture and lots of it from various translations. The emptiness of my failure caused me to begin seeking the Lord desperately and wholeheartedly, not just His word, not just prayers, but all of Him, God, my Lord. I needed Him to totally and completely bathe my spirit with Himself, His fullness (Ephesians 3:19) to cleanse me and start afresh. I craved to know Him... and Him alone. My being had become nothing but dry, dead bones. Desperate for breath, for life within my being, I had become as a deer longing for streams of cool, refreshing water (Psalm 42:1–2, author's paraphrase).

Thus, it was important for me to have a church that taught the significance of knowing the joy of the Lord and establishing an ongoing relationship with Him, not religious doctrine with rules and regulations, but the whole gospel according to the Word of God.

Why not just go back to the church Ken and I had attended before his death? Since the pastorate had changed at the church we had originally attended when first moving to Texas, Ken decided to take a friend up on his suggestion to attend his place of worship, which happened to be just down the road about a mile or so. Ken, even though heavily medicated, would drive his motorized scooter at the speed of about four miles per hour down our narrow and busy road to attend church services.

A flashback of Ken trudging down a lonely patch of highway and grassland nineteen years earlier (when our marriage was just beginning) came to mind while I crept along behind him on one of those trips. Only, this time I was trailing his scooter with its flashing hazard lights and praying for safety as well as healing. Wouldn't it be incredibly fabulous, I thought, if he could just ditch that scooter and run back to the car and slide into the driver's seat?

Having only attended our friend's church about four times, we hadn't even made a connection before it became necessary for Ken to be hospitalized again, thus there really wasn't a place for me to go back to. After all this time without a church home, a sense of spiritual homelessness had set in. After exploring various churches, I decided to visit the one church whose name had continued to be on my mind: Trinity Lighthouse, in Denison, Texas, staffed by Pastors Raymond and Brenda along with their daughter, Gwen England, and assistant pastors Brian and Sheryl Ulch.

Even though I was afraid of making a scene with a multitude of tears, I finally went, hoping to be invisible. Friendly greeters eyed my face and reached out to shake my hand. Thankfully, they didn't ask any questions, just welcomed me. Arriving a tad bit late, (I had headed for another place of worship that morning but while in route changed my mind), the sanctuary doors were closed. Slowly and quietly I opened the door, thinking no one would see me enter.

Sweet, inviting choruses led by an amazingly and spiritually sensitive youth team greeted me, beckoning me to enter God's peaceful sanctuary. This music was exactly what I longed to hear: songs I had already mentioned to the Lord that I would love to hear in a service, especially if that was the place of worship where I belonged.

As my eyes continued to adjust to the dimmed light, a bold contrast to the bright, sunny morning, I paused before continuing inside. Then, as I walked on into the sanctuary, suddenly, to my immense surprise a former colleague, with one swoop of her arm, led me to an available seat next to her. We still worked for the same school district but had different building assignments. I had no idea she attended this congregation. How strange, I thought, and how comforting it felt to be cared for at that particular moment. She simply handed me a box of Puffs and slipped her arm around my shoulder. Obviously, she was a friend sent from heaven. I didn't have to think; I could just soak in the Spirit of God. She even filled me in on all the studies and activities I would want to get involved in immediately. And she wrote them all down! This angel on earth knew exactly what I needed.

She presented two potential interests. The first opportunity was a home Bible study group, Kingdom Builders, which gathered every other Friday evening, and the other was the monthly women's group meeting coming up in just two days. For quite a month of Sundays, she took me under her wing. A number of Sundays later, she informed me she usually sat in the middle of the sanctuary, not on the far right where we first met. Hmmm, I thought. Had God placed her in that strategic spot just for me?

In addition to establishing a new church home and participating in a few Bible studies classes, I also wanted to collect a few more college credit hours. So when the 2009 school year closed for summer, I enrolled in three K–sixth grade continuing education classes back in Kansas at Friends University. Thankfully, I was able to stay with a dear friend during these days. Determined to keep my teaching options open, I was ready to do whatever it took. Should I ever return to my home state for employment in education, an active license would be crucial. Thus renewing my Kansas teaching license in a timely fashion meant I would need all of these credit hours in addition to the children's literature class I had already attended in the spring.

Being in class as a student again was indeed wonderful. It was familiar. It was refreshing. I enjoyed the people. I enjoyed the camaraderie. I enjoyed the learning environment. I enjoyed being away from Texas and back in my Kansas surroundings with friends from the past—that is until the third class.

Each course had had its own creative projects and presentations that students had to complete within two days, which was typically easy enough. However, by the time that third class was ending, fatigue had usurped my thinking, and my brain just stopped. Just like that, it quit. Needless to say, I seriously struggled with that final project. Not a single sensible idea would come to my mind; I could not comprehend anything. How was I to tie the content taught in the class together with the practicalities of classroom usage? Time had run out. Stressfully, our individual presentations were due.

Thankfully, the instructor didn't ask a lot of questions. I couldn't have answered them without a total meltdown of ever-flowing tears. She simply came alongside and gave me some much-needed suggestions and direction. Her empathy gave me just enough strength to complete the course satisfactorily. The Lord's compassion was definitely in that blessing.

Once back home in Texas, I still had to write the essay and complete the required activities for the children's literature course. Oh my. Without a shadow of doubt, it was only God who could have taken my shaken mind, ordered it with all the pertinent details about how to arrange a teaching session with a class of elementary students, put the necessary words down on paper, and finalize the efforts into three quality essays before the deadline! As I write this book, I see clearly now how the Lord, especially then, was providing for my every need. And I do believe the education classes did indeed assist with the beginnings of getting my mind back on track.

I've been told that God sees and bottles up all our tears (Psalm 56:8, author's paraphrase). Unquestionably, it must be an enormous bottle, for the first women's meeting I attended proved to be an extremely tearful one. All the women stood in a circle that evening to pray for whatever needs we had, but I could not pray, I could only think one word, "Lord," and that alone caused me to weep, and weep, drenching the paper towel I held. When the last tear had fallen that evening, I looked up and noticed I was practically the only one still standing. It was pretty obvious who needed prayer that night! Gathering up more courage, I later asked the leader of our gathering to pray with me. From her own firsthand experience with a recent grievous loss, she prayed mightily and effectively for me. Throughout the month following this gathering, the oppressive and weighted grieving began to subside, which gave me liberty once again. I could literally feel the heaviness of burdens lifting away. Psalm 3:3 declares God is the lifter of my head, and He holds up the hands that hang down. Oh, this is so wonderfully true.

I continued with Bible studies and ladies' meetings, and day by day, week by week, and month by month, the Lord was revealing His truth. God always reminded me, no matter what I was doing, when it was time for Kingdom Builders' Friday evening Bible study. The printed words "Bible Study" sort of flashed into my mind at that time. Because of that, my attendance at this Bible Study was never a problem. Since the Lord was saying, "Go," I thought I had better follow His direction. Once again, I was regaining lost ground and confidence in His word. Wonderful friendships with this seasoned and saintly group would grow as well. Furthermore, death had parted a number of these individuals from their spouses; they had walked ahead on this same path. I cherish each one of these dear, sweet saints.

"We have also obtained access through Him by faith ... and we rejoice in the hope of the glory of God." Romans 5:2 became a powerful turning point in my life. It proved to be extremely helpful in rediscovering confidence in Christ. As part of the topic of the evening study one night, after I had asked for something more to meditate upon, our leader gave me this verse to devote more perusal to. Another saintly lady joined in, saying, "That is pretty deep; it will take a lot of time." In essence, her words led me to spend much time studying that Scripture—each word individually. The gaping hole in my heart was being mended as I once again understood it is God himself who invites us to come into His presence. He gives us invitation, time and time again to access His grace and favor with His confidence; by faith we stand safely and firmly in Him.

Confidence! We all need confidence in Christ. My discovery of renewed confidence was a beginning and a step forward in the right direction. Thank You, dear Lord, for the presence of Your warmth and love within my being.

Another deeply influential study was, "Identity Theft" from Duane Sheriff Ministries. This was a twelve-week teaching series taught via CD and group discussion that takes the listener back to the beginning, to Satan's greatest crime against humanity, and explains why and how our identity in the Lord has been stolen. It explains why this identity is at risk and then powerfully builds spiritual concept upon concept telling who we truly are in Christ.

Through this course I learned we are deeply loved by the Lord, highly blessed and greatly favored. We are created in the righteousness of Christ, in His image. Christ paid the ultimate and grisly price for us on the cross, bearing our sins, our guilt, our diseases, our infirmities. He sealed our salvation for us forever. Through the blood of Jesus, God made us the head and not the tail, above and not below. Christ came to recover and restore humanity's true identity through being born again in Him, and we must discover that identity by the Spirit of God. We then become bold for Christ.

Gratefully, I praise the Lord for all the avenues He has provided and continues to make available for spiritual growth. However, another part of me continues to struggle with personal growth. Even these five years later, at the time of this writing, to actually say or even write the words, "widow" and/or "widower" leave me feeling as if I'm on some distant and deserted planet. Words like these still seem to be harsh, loveless words, and I refuse to be among the dead.

Yet, on the other hand, I have learned to shake off the effects of death and live again, and to live life more abundantly, more joyfully. Oh, Death, where is thy sting? Beyond doubt, it is found in the living, the ones wounded because of loss, because of departed loved ones. Yes, we will see each other again in heaven, for sure. Without a doubt, those who claim Jesus as Lord and Savior are with the Lord. In fact, we rejoice in the thought of their heavenly exuberance. But, while adjusting to life on this earth without them, their loss stings.

So, even though a bit of sting remains, basically the struggling has finally come to an end for me. Sweet surrender to the Lord's direction has begun. Deciding to live again was good; deciding to live life abundantly even better. I was free to follow whatever and however the Lord directed, one step at a time. But how?

Being ready to follow is one thing, but knowing how to follow is another question.

God's direction came a little at a time through continued Bible study, Bible reading, much prayer, time alone with the Lord, reading respected Christian authors' materials, and listening to pastors and Sunday school teachers. Through daily ordinary things, through the beauty of nature, through music, through babies, and through friends and acquaintances sharing their love of the Lord, I also heard God's voice.

God used people from all walks of life to help guide and direct my steps. "Keep your eyes on the Scripture, Mary Ann. That's where the proof is," a new friend would say. *Listen to what the Lord has to say* was my interpretation. This friend, a beautiful retired pastor's wife, greatly encouraged me with that sound advice. Her energetic and glowing demeanor of love from the Lord would fill the room each time she entered. She definitely sees more in me than what I can see within myself. Gratefully, she prays and continues to lift me higher.

Again, demonstration of God's love came through dear family friends who stayed in my life, praying on the sidelines. They didn't offer advice. They didn't ask questions. They were simply there. They gave us, the children and I, strength and encouragement with their presence and by standing with me. They, too, were grieving the loss of their friend. In essence, their nearness allowed some aspects of daily life to feel almost normal.

Abide in Christ by Andrew Murray, *The Practice of the Presence of God* by Brother Lawrence, and *Answers to Prayer* by George

Mueller were introduced to me at a time when I was readying my house for sale. I was planning, at that time and at the advice of a financial counselor, on moving back to Kansas, home, to be closer to family members.

In another manner, the gentleman who came to measure the square footage for new carpet found opportunity and shared his personal love for the Lord, his testimony. The tone in his voice as he spoke of his Lord was like none other I had ever heard; unmistakably, this dear person contained a pure, sweet love for the Lord. With his testimony captivating my attention, I could indeed, literally, see and sense the presence of the Lord spilling over from this man. As he walked the length of the house readying to leave, the spirit of the Lord followed him like a hot summer heat wave or a wake trailing the movement of a speeding boat on still waters. "Surely, your goodness and love will be with me all my life…" (Psalm 23:6 NCV) came to mind. A compelling desire to read God's Word was imprinted within me. And the fullness of God's presence permeated my home like a sweet aroma.

Later, during a neighborhood Bible study held in this man's home, the writings of Andrew Murray, especially *Abide in Christ* and *Waiting on God*, have crept sweetly into my heart and soul; my renewed faith in Jesus Christ has developed into a magnificent love story. Obviously, the more we allow Jesus to dwell in us, the more of Him we will desire. As that desire grows, the more He continues to complete us with His Spirit. And as we fully receive His Spirit, His wondrous presence genuinely develops a home within us.

After reading much of another book by Andrew Murray, *Andrew Murray on Prayer*, in addition to *Captivating: Unveiling the*

Mystery of a Woman's Soul by Staci and John Eldredge, my eyes have been opened to a marvelous understanding concerning God's unfathomable love for us. Our heavenly Father, our husband, romances us with every opportunity available. He continually shows us His love through every facet of life.

Daily, the Lord embraces me with His grand splendor, each morning with the majestic sunrise and each evening with the beauty of the sunset. He reveals Himself as He encapsulates me in a warm cocoon with each glorious ray of light. And then, each night, He sweetly layers my face with kisses from each gleaming star. May I say that it is indeed His *glory* that fills the earth and the heavens with such awesomeness? And to think He has always been right there, showing all of mankind Himself since long before I was ever born, and I'm just now, in these later years of life, absorbing His presence! God is healing my soul. Jesus is a love like no other.

Thankfully, my frustration and not understanding Ken's death has begun to dwindle. Even though I knew, from deep within, that the Lord was literally carrying me through this entire trauma, I first began to recognize the truth through His revelation of amazing gentleness, acceptance, and pure love for me. He embraced each inner fracture, the wounds of my soul, and filled the multiple layers afresh with His soothing Holy Spirit. Tenderly, He poured the healing balm of Gilead throughout the crevices and down into the depths of the abyss, soothing my woundedness. He covered me with the healing wings of Jesus. And, as with dry bones in the desert, He infused His very breath of life softly and ever so gently into my broken, disparaging spirit (Ezekiel 37:1–6, author's paraphrase). I underwent a living restoration measure by measure, and even today, I continue to realize a generous renovation within my soul and spirit.

Much like an uncomely mound of clay placed on the sculpting wheel before the master artist, welcoming renewal of spirit is imminent for my heart. With knowing hands the Master gently but firmly and meticulously begins the journey of crafting a new vessel especially suited to meet only His purposes. After an excruciatingly intense and rather lengthy firing process, He has made me stronger and much more resilient than ever before. The Lord says we are to wait upon Him regardless of discomfort. Frankly, that is all I am capable of doing; even then, I am only able to because He works it in me.

Finally, the artist produces His palette of heavenly hues. I keep my heart turned toward Him, waiting. The Master continues to exquisitely fashion me with His most radiant of sunrise splendor. He nudges my heart expectantly. I open my eyes, recognizing that true to His word, He has illuminated the layers of my heart and soul with His Glory and the light of heaven. I am made new, in His likeness! Truly, Jesus has immersed me in His love, uniquely permeating my spirit and soul, to become like Him.

Grieving is only for a time; *joy* unspeakable does come after the night of mourning. In His time, He does make all things splendidly beautiful.

As I stated earlier, it's not that I'm troubled now with Ken dying and being in heaven. Whether he died from sheer exhaustion in the fight for earthly life, simple submission to death, or surrendering to heaven's call, it doesn't matter. Ken's life is not lost; he has gained everything. Rather, it's the unanswered prayer that still burns in my soul. Why was our prayer *not* answered with our expectation?

"Is anyone among you sick? You should call for the elders of the church, and they should pray over him after anointing him with olive oil in the name of the Lord. The prayer of faith will save the sick person, and the Lord will restore him to health; if he has committed sins, he will be forgiven" (James 5:14–15). We did exactly that. Ken and I made an eleven-hour round-trip mission especially for this purpose.

James 4:3 states, "You ask and don't receive because you ask with wrong motives." What was our motive? Yet, Mathew 7:7–8 states, "Keep asking and it shall be given you; keep searching, and you will find; keep knocking, and the door will be opened to you. For everyone who asks receives; and the one who searches finds; and to the one who knocks it will be opened."

Other Scripture verses include encouraging words for healing as well.

"A man shall be satisfied with good by the words of his mouth ..." (Proverbs 12:14).

"Then He touched their eyes, saying, 'Let it be done for you according to your faith!'" (Matthew 9:29)

"I assure you: If anyone says to this mountain, 'Be lifted up and thrown into the sea,' and does not doubt in his heart, but believes that what he says will happen, it will be done for him" (Mark 11:23).

"If you ask Me anything in My name, I will do it" (John 14: 14).

"[T]hey will lay hands on the sick, and they will get well" (Mark 16: 18).

"[F]or I am Yahweh who heals you" (Exodus15:26).

"He forgives all your sin; and heals all your diseases" (Psalm 103:3).

"But He was pierced because of our transgressions, crushed because of our iniquities; punishment for our peace was on Him, and we are healed by His wounds" (Isaiah 53:5).

"He Himself bore our sins in His body on the tree, so that, having died to sins, we might live for righteousness, you have been healed by His wounds" (1 Peter 2:24).

"I will not die, but I will live and proclaim what the Lord has done" (Psalm 118:17).

"Look, I am about to do something new; even now it is coming. Do you not see it? Indeed, I will make a way in the wilderness, rivers in the desert" (Isaiah 43:19).

"The Angel of the Lord encamps around those who fear Him, and rescues them" (Psalm 34:7).

"I will be with you when you pass through the waters, and when you pass through the rivers, they will not overwhelm you. You will not be scorched when you walk through the fire, and the flame will not burn you" (Isaiah 43:2).

"Do not fear, for I am with you; do not be afraid, for I am your God. I will strengthen you;

I will help you; I will hold on to you with MY
righteous right hand" (Isaiah 41:10).

There are many more verses from which to claim and decree
physical healing. Did we not believe enough? Was our faith faulty?
Did we put God in a box?

$$\wp$$

As I seriously examine my heart, as painful as it is, I find
myself lacking and assuming. Even though we believed, even
though we prayed, even though we recited Scriptures, even
though we listened to healing Scriptures on CD, even though
we read about other people and their healings, even though we
did all we could do, were we not importunate, persistently and
strongly urgent, enough in our belief?

Sadly, I believe we depended more upon our own strength
than God's power. It was *us* doing all *we* could do, believing all
we could believe. We were waiting for God to cast His healing
upon Ken with our own expectations. We believed it was God's
will for all people to live in health and therefore just knew He
would heal again. But did we soak up God's power and honestly
bask in His presence? There didn't seem to be enough time for
soaking His Word into our spirits. Life, with much to care for, was
tremendously stressful. So we took God's Word and manipulated
it, used it toward our own purposes.

Even though we may have had a glimpse of what God
intended, perhaps we completed it with our own human
understanding instead of applying spiritual principals to what

we did understand. Thus, we inadvertently allowed and followed deception.

What I do know with confidence, at this time, is God does know the plans and thoughts He has for His children to bring us good and not evil and to give us hope in His salvation. When we search for God with all our hearts as a vital necessity, we do find Him (Jeremiah 29:11–13, author's paraphrase).

Murray presents it like this:

> It is the adoring worship of God—the waiting on Him and for Him in the deep silence of soul that yields itself for God to reveal Himself—that the capacity for knowing and trusting God will be developed. As we take His Word from the blessed Book and ask Him to speak it to us with His living, loving voice, the power to believe and receive the Word as God's own word to us will emerge in us. It is in prayer in living contact with God in living faith, that faith will become strong in us. It is God—the living God—into whom our faith must strike its roots deeply and broadly. Then it will be strong enough to remove mountains and cast out devils. (*Andrew Murray on Prayer*, 373)

Could it be that God is more interested in our state of abiding in Him than He is in our physical comfort or health? Could it be in God's infinite wisdom to stir up our comfortable nest and push us out and over the precipice, all while fear trembles in our hearts, and with eyes tightly closed, we feel the downward plummet?

Then as if alight on eagles' wings, He catches us and carries us up into His higher planes. Is it so He can replace our fear, our weakness, our helplessness, our misunderstanding with Himself? Does He put us in a place where we have no choice but to wait on Him? And, when we trust Him more, it seems He again stirs the nest, causing us to plunge headlong from our trusted perch only to find ourselves being nestled again onto His wings. Is this how He teaches us to wait upon Him? Is this a process of how we learn faith? Murray says yes (Andrew Murray on Prayer, p. 283–284, author's paraphrase). Oh, what love the Lord has for us, His children!

But isn't it God's plan for each of us to live whole and in good health? Did Jesus heal everyone among the sick? I cannot begin to come up with all the answers. For us, perhaps we indeed believed in the words of Scripture, but as I examine those days of Ken's final illness more closely, I genuinely believe we were not totaling trusting the author of those words. Yes, we repeated healing Scriptures every day; we believed, but perhaps like one who holds a rabbit's foot, we had our lucky charm. Obviously we were not in touch with the power behind the words. Had we simply borrowed words of Scripture from others who successfully beat their illnesses? Unknowingly, we must not have had the heart of God in our grasp. And, I see now, we also leaned on the prayers given by others more than what we gave from our own hearts and spirits.

When Ken had his first round of cancer, I willed with all my being that he would be healed and live as if my very existence depended upon it. I walked in many Scriptures of healing words that flew off the pages and clung to the interior of my heart and soul.

But during the second round years later with pancreatic cancer, I assumed God would just heal him as He had before. Honestly, my prayers were as if I was too tired to pray diligently and with importunance, being emphatically persistent. I couldn't for whatever reason muster the "will" to pray effectively enough with this disease.

Could that have been because my attitude was one of "because I believed it, surely God is obligated to perform it"? How foolish I feel about that mind-set now. Our beliefs must not be reduced to a formula, just repeated Scriptures. Rather, our hearts must make the connection; the Word must come alive within us. We must be in agreement with what the Lord has planned. Even though we put our faith in the Word, our faith must first be built on our personal relationships with the Lord. We must be careful not to be caught in the trap of believing only what we choose at the expense of truth. Furthermore, we cannot put God in a box. Just because He acted a certain way with an issue in our lives once or with other individuals, doesn't mean He'll do it again in that same manner. We must follow Him and be alert to His direction, instead of expecting Him to follow our logic, our beliefs, and our desires.

Furthermore, as I wrote this message, I saw I had gotten so caught up in the urgent demands of care giving, of being in control of my husband's life care, that I perhaps thought *I* could cover Ken's lack of faith, if indeed there was a lack. Additionally, if *I* took good enough care of him, surely he would live. That isn't a pretty picture, but is most likely true.

Andrew Murray's definition of faith is: "the ear that has heard God say what He will do and the eye that has seen Him doing it"

(*Andrew Murray on Prayer*, p. 362). Hebrews 11:1 states that faith is the reality of what is hoped for, the proof of what is not seen. We wanted this type of faith. But could it be our faith, Ken's faith, was weakened? Could it be he felt he was unworthy of healing? On one occasion, he did state that he felt this illness was to the death. Was he too tired of fighting life's harassing onslaughts? I couldn't accept that thought, though. I insisted God was healing him.

Mueller states faith with every fresh trial either increases by trusting God, thus getting help, or decreases by not trusting Him; then there is less and less power of looking simply and directly to the Lord. (*Answers to Prayer*, George Mueller, pg. 47)

Spiritually, we can do nothing in and of ourselves. By God's spirit alone we live and move and have our being and are able to follow His leading. It is imperative we empty ourselves of us and allow God to fill His holy temple within us with His words, His spirit, His being, and His love.

ॐ

January 22, 2011. Three days before the second anniversary of Ken's going home, a dream vividly unfolded while I slept.

An old, white-framed house, Victorian in style, from which paint had long ago peeled away, sat under the canopy of well-established lofty green shade trees basking in the gentle, warm breeze. Tall, untamed shrubbery outlined the once-ornate side porch. An unknown person and I slipped through to enter the rather dilapidated, unkempt, and abandoned home. Inside, a stream of light meandered drowsily into the living room from the dusty windowpanes. Softly, a sunbeam highlighted a smudged, ornately framed oval photograph of a precious loved one -a sweet memory of long ago. Upon a deftly crocheted beige doily, it sat on a side table under the window and had been left in silence. Highlights from this window also poured into the otherwise darken and shadowy adjoining room. Surprisingly, even though dusty, warm, and humid, this intriguingly charming house was without musty, moldy odors. Instead, a hint of a fresh floral aroma permeated the air, perhaps from the cluster of antique rosebushes outside the dining room window.

Bona fide living people had lived in this long-ago attractive home. Sudden mysterious events had taken place. "Grandmom" needed to leave, to relocate quickly. She left behind several personal belongings. Now, her children, their urgent difficulties sent her running back into this home for their good; she had to find something.

Before leaving, this distantly familiar person, who I recognized as being from school and I the librarian, needed me to accompany her to the house. While gingerly stepping soundlessly up the staircase she vanished, leaving me alone to look about. Gritty with dust the items left were now only a shadow of their original state. Spiders were quietly watching, guarding, proudly sitting here and there, as well as resting in a large, brown paper grocery bag filled with treasured items unintentionally, it seemed, left behind. My heart ached to hold and examine those little trophies, possibly souvenirs. Intending to reach into this cache, I thoughtfully reconsidered at the sight of these arachnids. Cobwebs and their creators seemed to be protecting this elusive treasure.

The carpet appeared to be quite clean and new, soft beige or tan in color, yet with closer examination, I found crawdads, little crabs, and snails crawling all over it and across my shoes! I stepped carefully, not injuring a single one. Initially, a fleeting thought came to mind, about asking to have a portion of the carpet placed in my home since it obviously was not needed in this old house. But I didn't. Insects and crustaceans, I could see, obviously had put their claim on it.

I was conscious now that these left-behind items were sacred. They all belonged to the sacredness of this era and place. I wanted to keep those things, those artifacts of temporal value, move them into the new place. Keep them with me. I was then reminded of another scene where the stone had rolled away. Jesus emerged from His tomb with resurrection power alive and well. New life in Him was brilliantly illuminated! As the dream continued I realized the old does not belong with the new, just like new wine skins versus old wine skins. Don't earnestly remember the past, look to the future; don't you perceive that I am doing a new thing? (Isaiah 43: 18–19, author's paraphrase)

In this moment, I notice an open, enlarged, double doorway ahead to my right from which another light came into view; a lustrous, gleaming, yellow light was beckoning me to come closer. Inquisitively, I stepped across the threshold. Such brilliant, bright, bustling, energetic life and glorious light embraced me, engulfing me in all its glory, filling my very being, my soul and spirit alike. Alive, in the present moment, is where I am to be.

We do not belong there in the past. For the things as well as our loved ones from the past belong not to us. We intrude into their sanctum when we go back to snoop around and desire to take things from then into the now. Our presence disrupts the souls and things from the sanctuary of these people, their own sacred and holy sanctum. All belongs to them then, and it continues to belong to them, even now, in the present.

We don't necessarily close the door, say goodbye, or even try to forget; we simply and quietly move from them, the soul ties and souvenirs, into an adjacent sanctum, prepared by God for us individually, just as holy, just as sacred, just as unfeigned. Thus, we leave the heart of yesteryears safe and snug in the "home," in the arms of the Lord. Knowing both are sacred, we have the freedom to subsequently take the next step ahead into the fullness of God's glory light with confidence and joyful exuberance!

✍

So why did I so desperately need to hold on to Ken? Most likely it was because of unfulfilled promises and dreams. He still had a testimony to share; he wanted to be involved in a prison ministry, to make a difference in a wayward and struggling life. My prayer for him was to actively serve the Lord with his whole heart, soul, mind, and body, living with joy by the hand of the Lord. It didn't seem as if it was time for him to leave. It didn't seem as if he had finished the race. My heart sensed there was much more to come from his life.

God has a plan, of course, for each of our lives; obviously His plan is not always our plan. His thoughts are not like our thoughts; His ways are much higher than ours (Isaiah 55: 8–9, author's paraphrase).

Furthermore, heaven is the believers' destination, our home. Today, I simply rejoice in knowing Ken is entirely healed and gloriously joyful before the throne of God, full of praise and worship, a stark contrast to his earthly life! Vince Gill's popular song, "Go Rest High on That Mountain," a favorite of Ken's, is perfectly fitting as his life was indeed full of struggles.

At the time of this writing it has been almost five years since Ken's entrance into heaven. I'm so thankful for all the individuals God has brought onto my path since his death. They have walked with me and have lovingly and patiently poured Christ into me, many of them totally unaware of their input. Like a thirsty sponge, not a drop of this precious love has escaped me.

Thankfully, God continues to lead and direct my life, moving me on into an exciting and fulfilling course. Living in God's presence is wonderfully thrilling and most joyful. An abundance of glorious blessings lie ahead because Jesus is all in all. I have been set free!

With a heart of gratitude I can humbly share with you this thought. As I now spend time with the Lord, I'm beginning to sense strong roots flourishing out from my feet into a thick, solid foundation along with tiny little fruits dangling from my fingertips. Praise God!

Jesus is a love like no other! Smoothly, like fluid ink, these words have poured out onto the pages. May I share with you this wonderfully amazing happening as I placed the exclamation point at the end of the previous sentence? The Lord's loving hands ever so gently held my heart and spirit in the most holy and all-consuming powerfully warm embrace!

Perhaps He, the Lord, was saying, "Well done. I love you too!" Once again, let me say, "Jesus truly is a love like no other!"

Works Cited

Burke, Billy, *Breaking Soul Ties*. Billy Burke World Outreach. 2003. CD Series

Eldredge, John and Stasi. *Captivating: Unveiling the Mystery of a Woman's Soul*. Nashville: Thomas Nelson, Inc. 2005.

Eldredge, John. *Wild at Heart: Discovering the Secret of a Man's Soul*. Nashville: Thomas Nelson, Inc. 2001.

Muller, George. *Answers to Prayer*. George Mueller's Narratives Compiled by E. C. Brooks. Rosalie De Rosset, General Editor. Chicago: Moody Publishers, 2007.

Murray, Andrew. *Andrew Murray on Prayer*. New Kensington, PA: Whitaker House, 1998.

Sheriff, Duane. "A Crime Against Humanity." *Identity Theft, Who Am I*, set I. Duane Sheriff Ministries. 2009. CD series.

Sheriff, Duane. "Discovering & Recovering Your True Identity." *Identity Theft, Who Am I*, set II. Duane Sheriff Ministries. 2009. CD series.

You are welcome to contact

Mary Berry

at the following addresses

PO Box 1764

Sherman, TX 75091

www.Jesusalovelikenoother.com

and/or

maryberry@jesusalovelikenoother.com